Healing
Grief

OTHER BOOKS BY JAMES VAN PRAAGH

Talking to Heaven (Piatkus)
Reaching to Heaven (Piatkus)

JAMES VAN PRAAGH

Healing
Grief

RECLAIMING LIFE AFTER
ANY LOSS

PIATKUS

First published in 2000 in the USA by
Dutton, a member of Penguin Putnam, Inc.

Published in the UK in 2000 by
Judy Piatkus (Publishers) Limited
5 Windmill Street
London W1T 2JA
e-mail: *info@piatkus.co.uk*

For the latest news and information on all our
titles, visit our website at www.piatkus.co.uk

The moral right of the author has been asserted

*A catalogue record for this book is available
from the British Library*

ISBN 0 7499 2149 8

Printed and bound in Great Britain by
Butler & Tanner Ltd, Frome and London

*I dedicate this book to all who have experienced a life-altering loss.
It is my hope that in some small way, the words printed on these pages
will help calm your storm and make way for a sunny tomorrow.*

CONTENTS

ACKNOWLEDGMENTS

I am not only blessed to interact with heavenly angels, but am fortunate to meet earthly ones as well. Here are just a few who have guided and assisted me in bringing this book to you:

Allan Van Praagh—Thank you, Dad, for believing in me. You have taught me that kindness and love are the only ways to make a heart grow.

Lynn, Michael, and Maura—We each walk our own path, but it is comforting to know we are sharing the destiny together.

Linda Carwin Thomchin—Your patience, grace, and fortitude have kept me going. Thank you for always giving my words that extra ring.

Brian Preston—You make my heart overflow. Thank you for the peace and love you have brought to my life.

Bill and Donna Moller, Marie Levine, Joerdie and Eric Fisher, members of The Compassionate Friends, and all of those parents who have shared your heartfelt pain. Thank you for being a source of courage, strength, and knowledge to so many. I am forever grateful for your assistance in spreading heaven's eternal message.

Peter Redgrove—You are a soulful friend and teacher. Thank you for always encouraging me that nothing is impossible.

Eby "Jorge" Kaba—Your friendship, loyalty, and kindness can only be measured by the brightness of the stars. Only you know how to make them shine.

Joan Miller—Thank you for your random acts of kindness and a smile to match.

Dorothea Delgado—You are my "soul sister" and "Earth mother." Thank you for sharing this circle of life.

Wendy Rosenthal—My life has not been the same since you touched me with your joyful enthusiasm and your unique zest for life.

To everyone I have met through readings, lectures, book tours, chats, seminars, trips, and letters. Thank you, kind souls, for connecting with me and recognizing the truth within yourselves.

INTRODUCTION

*F*or many years I have been blessed to be an instrument for people to contact their loved ones on the other side. As I look back on these experiences, I realize that the unique encounters with the spiritual realms, together with my own life's lessons, were part of the preparation of writing the book you are about to read. As someone who has been enlightened by the insightful perspectives of those who have crossed onto the shores of the spiritual lands, I share this guide with you to assist in your healing of grief and loss.

I do not profess to be an expert in the fields of psychology or grief therapy, yet this book offers therapeutic remedies that I believe are beneficial to all. As human beings, we need a structure of psychological understanding to which we can relate. However, my approach to the grieving process incorporates resources of a spiritual nature, and it is from this unique perspective that I present the information.

As a professional medium for most of my adult life, I have witnessed many tragic situations. I have listened intensely for thousands of hours to the subtle whispers between our earthly world and the finer etheric world of spirit. I have miraculously witnessed spirit's golden words of light and wisdom break down stone-hardened hearts of grief and give life back to the mournful. I now wish to share with you these various insights in the hope that you will be touched by the awareness of eternal life so that you do not have to go through the rest of your days groping blindly in sorrow and pain. It is my deepest desire that this new perspective will initiate an opening to your own spiritual discovery and bring peace of mind and a new sense of purpose to your life.

The book is divided into four sections and offers various methods of facing loss and understanding grief in healthy and beneficial ways. In the first part, "The Process," I discuss the stages of grief, how we grieve, and what to expect as you go through the process. The second part, entitled "When Someone You Love Dies," concerns the loss of loved ones—parents, partners, children, grandparents, siblings, and friends. Like you, I have had my own share of tragedies, and I discuss my personal experiences of death, loss, and grief, along with those who have sought my assistance in their darkest hours. Also included are healing guidelines that will help you to make healthy choices and give you the encouragement to carry on. In the next section of the book, "Losses of a Different Kind," I describe losses that are not as obvious as death, such as divorce, mid-life crisis, coping with a terminal illness, losing our home or job, aging, and the loss of a pet. We may not be aware that everyday situations like these are also cause for grieving, and often we do not progress in life because we have suppressed feelings when these losses occur. The final part of the book, "Reclaiming Your Life," is devoted to various exercises, meditations, and mental processes that you can use to clarify unresolved issues and cope with unwanted feelings like guilt, anger, and depression. Also included are questions and answers about the spirit world and the grieving process.

The game of life is filled with twists and turns. Along the way I have found it invaluable to take time out every now and then and reflect upon certain events. These are the "moments" that make us unique beings. When thinking about moments of the past, I look to see if I have lived or experienced them fully. In this way I can review the choices I have made and recognize the value each of these moments has to offer. It is upon such reflection that I have come to an understanding that my life is the result of the choices I have made at each particular moment. The twists and turns served as my teachers on the ever winding road to spiritual wisdom.

By reading the narration and experiences contained within, you may begin to recognize your loss, beyond the pain and sadness it brings, as an opportunity to involve yourself fully in life. By doing so, each day you, too, can become aware of the "moments" of your life and, with confidence, have a desire to make every one count.

One of your moments is about to begin.

PART I

The Process

GRIEF AND LOSS

*N*o matter where we live or what language we speak, we share a common experience with everyone else on the planet—the loss of someone or something close to us. Loss can be sudden, without warning, or predictable, and still we are unable to prevent it from happening. All loss brings up feelings and memories, and for some these experiences may seem uneventful, while for others such loss changes the course of their lives forever. When someone or something is gone from our lives, we experience an array of physical, emotional, and spiritual sensations known as grief. Webster's Dictionary defines grief as "a deep and poignant distress caused by or as if by bereavement; a cause of such suffering; a mishap, misadventure, trouble, annoyance; an unfortunate outcome: disaster."

Why is there grief and why do we have to go through it? Grief serves a very important purpose. It is a reaction to our loss. It represents our underlying sense of insecurity. Our fears of abandonment and feelings of vulnerability rise to the surface, forcing us to face them. The world upon which we predicated our belief systems, goals, and our lives in general is suddenly out of control. We feel scared and exposed. Most of us don't want to deal with or feel these negative emotions, and yet they are just as relevant and as important to our well-being as our positive feelings. We need both positive and negative to be fully human. It has been said that one would never appreciate the positive emotions if he never knew of the negative ones. That is why it is so important to face negative emotions and experience them because by doing so, we build trust and confidence within ourselves. The worst thing we can do is to deny and repress them altogether. This only delays our spiritual growth.

Another factor to keep in mind is that grief is not an illness from which we recover. It is not merely one thing, but a process of feelings and physical conditions, and one cannot judge how much grief is enough grief. You should never feel pressured as to how you are supposed to grieve, for there is no right or wrong way. It is important to remember that there are healthy and constructive ways to go through the grieving process, as well as destructive and unhealthy ones, which can lead to more suffering.

Every time a loved one dies, we lose a little hope of a better future. A human being has been torn from our lives. A relationship is cut off in one swift blow. We feel frustrated, angry, sad, and confused. We feel regret for things undone and words unsaid. We wonder why the innocent or good die young, and the good-for-nothings live too long. Grieving for our loved ones is not an intellectual process. We have to learn to understand our own feelings and come to peace with the situation. Even when a personality or a celebrity dies, we go through a grieving process. It all depends on how much vested interest we had in such a person. We may experience his or her death as a personal loss. When John Kennedy Jr. died, many people who didn't know him cried on his behalf. His death brought up memories of his father, uncle, mother, and an era that seemed simpler. At times like these we mourn the loss of what might have been, especially if we feel that life is passing us by too quickly. We also feel our own fragility as humans because we don't know when our time will come. And because death is scary and unknown, we grieve our own mortality.

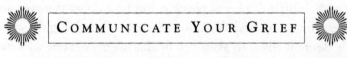

COMMUNICATE YOUR GRIEF

At the onset of any loss, our first reactions are usually shock or disbelief. After a while we come to the realization of our loss, and our feelings turn to sadness, anger, loneliness, guilt, despair, and a whole array of emotions, bodily ills, and other physical conditions. Sometimes our grief seems like an endless process, as if we were trapped in an abyss of darkness without the possibility of escape. Yet loss and grief are frequent occurrences, and most of us are ill prepared to handle them. First of all, we are not used to talking about our grief. Instead, we keep our thoughts and feelings to ourselves, or we rush to discard or ignore the pain we feel. Second, we often rationalize, "If I don't think about it, it will go away." As a society, we do little

to help each other understand the effect of loss or even to allow individuals the time necessary to recognize the hurt, sadness, and confusion they feel.

Because we as a society would rather hide and deny death
and loss, instead of embracing it and becoming educated about
it, we have never been properly taught how to grieve. Therefore, when an event like a death or the onset of a terminal illness occurs, we don't have the necessary tools with which to
deal with the situation. We feel that denying its existence is
easier because the pain is too unbearable. However, if we possess an awareness of grief and the emotions born of it, we will
be that much better prepared to deal with it in a positive, constructive manner and to face it with less fear and anxiety.

Grieving is a natural process of life, and as a process, it takes
time to get through. Instead of allowing ourselves the opportunity to break through the grief barrier and reconstruct our
lives with a sense of renewal and hope, we expect to get over
it with as little display as possible. But how do we get over our
grief without an understanding of what we are going through?
My desire really is to assist you by sharing my experiences and
the experiences of others who have gone through, and continue to go through, the grieving process. I will also give you
ways and methods from a spiritual point of view to observe
your own grief, so you can come out of the pain and confusion
with an entirely new perspective. Your change in attitude may
help you to become a totally whole and loving person. Because
you will be learning immeasurable insights about yourself and
others, you can, in turn, take the steps necessary to create a
happier and more fulfilling life for yourself.

The only way to avoid grief is to avoid life, and live without
love. Grieving is very human. It's a process that can heal our
emotional upheaval and mental uncertainty. Everyone feels
various degrees of anguish and suffering during the process,

and these feelings are natural and normal. Healthy grieving is taking responsibility for your own life. In order to continue life in any meaningful way, you must allow yourself to grieve.

One of the first important steps in acknowledging your sense of loss is to say good-bye to your loved ones. Many people refuse to say good-bye because they feel that if they do, they are dismissing the person or ending any opportunity to speak with him or her again. Saying good-bye helps us to realize that this person is only gone physically. The mind needs to have some sort of closure. In our culture, we have created certain rituals for saying good-bye. We attend a funeral or hold a memorial service. We light candles in churches or say prayers for the dead. These rituals are necessary for us as humans. Many a spirit has communicated how pleased it was to see family members present at its funeral. A spirit will usually stay around for such a ceremony. Such a ritual not only helps the living to readjust, but also helps the spirit to recognize that it is no longer part of the physical plane. No matter how we say good-bye, whether it is at a formal memorial or in the privacy of our own hearts, it is important that we do it. Remember that a spirit never dies. We can console ourselves with the knowledge that our loved ones are always around us. We can talk with them, and they will hear us. Remember, too, that life is constantly changing, and *nothing is ever lost*. What was only turns into something else.

It is also necessary to reach closure when other types of losses occur. We must be able to say good-bye to a variety of situations and circumstances that are no longer part of our daily life. Saying good-bye is never easy but often necessary. There comes a time when we have to close a door on some chapter of our lives and come to a completion in our minds. All grief needs to be felt and realized. We need to accept the loss in order to begin the healing process. If we don't grieve,

we remain stagnant and carry the burden of unfinished business with us throughout life. Unprocessed grief affects our life
decisions and colors every situation that we encounter. By repressing our true feelings, we push the pain deeper. Therefore,
we can never really live life to its fullest potential. Instead, we
merely exist.

A SPIRITUAL PERSPECTIVE

When the body is shed and we cross over to the spirit world,
we open the door to eternal life. It is there that we discover
that we are spiritual beings having human experiences. You
will find through the stories presented in this book that we are
on this earth to evolve and develop spiritually. In order to do
so, we make choices before incarnating into our physical bodies to place ourselves in various situations in order to grow.
Some of the situations may be painful: we lose a child, or we go
through a divorce. We get ill and incapacitated. We lose our
home and all our possessions. Some situations may be less distressing but disturbing nevertheless. Our children grow up and
move away. We grow old alone without our friends, or we
never reach our goal or dream. These lessons are all part of the
incredible growth and understanding that a soul creates for itself. You must remember that you are taking part in a spiritual
action, not just a physical one. You are playing your part to
evolve to the next phase of your spiritual development. Perhaps you have to fulfill a karmic obligation with another person. Perhaps you have to change certain beliefs about your life,
or you have to learn to control your anger. Maybe you have to
master self-confidence and self-esteem. Perhaps, too, you have
decided to sacrifice your needs for someone else. No matter

what the reasons, the soul always makes the choice to go through an experience while on earth. If we keep this in mind, we will come to an awareness that life is a continuous process, and that we will come into the physical and go out again. This is just one of many lifetimes of our spiritual journey. There is a reason and purpose for your being alive right now. Let your grief become an opportunity for your soul to grow.

The conditions of grieving are common to everyone, as you will read in the next chapter about the stages of grief. We always have the choice either to move forward with optimism or stay stuck in sorrow.

2

THE GRIEVING
PROCESS

*L*ife can be measured only by the experiences we accumulate on this earth.
By its very nature, life is a potpourri of events
that are filtered through our emotional,
physical, mental, and spiritual selves. The
purpose of life is to learn to appreciate these
various aspects of ourselves. As we experience life's ups and downs, hopefully we grow
in the knowledge and wisdom of ourselves as
loving, spiritual beings.

An important and painful part of the life
experience is grief, which is a natural consequence of loss. Invariably, it is a part of life.
The degree of pain and discomfort associated with grief will vary depending on the
degree of the loss and our relationship with

the loss, whether it is a loved one, a circumstance, or a pet. Each person is impacted differently and reacts in his or her own distinct way.

In my first book, *Talking to Heaven*, I detailed the initial re-actions one goes through during a loss. Now I would like to ex-pand on that list and incorporate within it the stages of grief.

THE STAGES OF GRIEF

When reviewing and using these stages as a reference, you should realize that all of them are healthy, and each stage may be experienced in different ways and at different times. There are no rules or set regimen that accompany these feelings or stages. A person may get stuck in one stage and not be able to move on to the next. Quite frequently these stages may even blend together, or one may experience several stages of grief at different periods of time. Every person has his or her own agenda and timetable from which to work, and therefore each will experience the various stages in a unique way. One must have patience and realize that grieving is a process. We are all "works in progress" on our journey through life, and nothing can be accomplished overnight.

Many go through grieving on their own, but there are also those who cannot cope and need help or guidance from others. A therapist, facilitator, family member or friend can play an important part in your healing process. These outside helpers can encourage you to keep going, and share in your inner thoughts and feelings. So many times, all that a person needs is to talk to someone. He or she is not looking for someone to judge or talk back, but merely to listen. Listening helps a griev-ing person to verbalize or to express his or her hurt. And even though the situation of loss varies, such as losing a spouse to losing a job, the process is the same. Again, the degree to which we are affected will depend on how deeply we feel the loss.

Shock

The first reaction to a loss is total disbelief. A person is rarely prepared for the event, and it takes him or her completely by surprise. Your world is thrown upside down, and you feel completely out of control. Whether the death is a sudden one or caused by a long, lasting illness, the shock of finality remains the same. The news of a loss can paralyze even the strongest among us. The emotional overload is so great that you feel as if you were hit by a truck.

This first stage of grief is a time when we usually cannot understand the impact of what has just happened and cannot fathom it as being real. We are stunned. We feel ourselves going numb. Just as the body goes into shock after a severe accident, the mind goes into shock in order to deal with extreme emotional upheaval. In our minds, we may say phrases over and over again like, *I can't believe it*, or *He couldn't be dead*, or *This couldn't be happening*. It is important to realize that you are not going crazy, and that your response is indeed normal. Your shock could last from as little as a few hours to as much as a few months. You may feel as if you are living through a real-life nightmare as you keep repeating, *It can't be true*. The numbness is temporary, but the shock can go on for some time.

When people are in shock, many times they act like robots, as though they are just going through the motions. One will often lose a sense of awareness of doing everyday tasks. Also, it is quite common to go through memory lapses. Even minor things that you take for granted seem to fade away. We may misplace items or forget details. People talk to us, but we don't hear what they are saying. We can't make any plans for tomorrow, never mind the future. It's as if our bodies are going through slow motion. These reactions are all part of the intense shock you are feeling.

Shock is more or less a defense mechanism. When we are not able to deal with our emotional state at the moment, shock takes over to help us get through the few days following the devastating event so that we do not feel the full impact of the death or changed circumstances. After the shock and numbness begin to wear off, we then begin to understand the reality of the situation. But we will still find ourselves saying, *I can't believe it*. That is because we are dealing with a situation that is totally different, and we still have to get used to a new way of life.

Denial

Denial is a close associate of shock. These two reactions almost emerge in tandem with each other. Denial, like shock, acts as a buffer to the reality of the situation. When we are in denial, we are prevented from dealing with the feelings of our newfound condition. Because we are so used to the people in our lives, or our old patterns and situations, when something changes, we don't want to accept it. Instead, we deny its existence. The longer we are in denial, the longer we avoid facing our grief.

There are different levels of denial, depending upon the relationship the aggrieved has had with the loss. Denial remains a part of our lives until we are able to acknowledge our loss and go through grief. Many who stay in denial begin to find other ways to numb their pain, using alcohol and drugs. In the case of divorce, some people jump right into another relationship and don't give themselves the time necessary to go through the grieving process. They stay in denial because they do not want to deal with all the pain and sadness of their ordeal.

When bad situations arise, it is quite common to find other distractions or fantasies to keep our minds busy. This, too, keeps us from confronting our pain. We pretend that if we don't think about something, it will go away, and everything will get back to normal. We play mind games with ourselves. Sooner or later we have to wake up from our fantasy if we want to get on with our lives. The longer we stay in denial, the more our game becomes a cruel nightmare. Eventually, reality does set in.

I know we live in a society built on escapism and fantasy. Denial seems like a good way to deal with many of the unpleasant issues existing in our world. We don't like to think of them and would rather avoid them altogether. We don't like feeling helpless and hopeless. It's not the agenda that society advocates. No one teaches us what to do, or how to feel or behave, when life-altering changes occur. We are not supposed to appear weak or vulnerable. Heaven forbid if we should cry. These are signs of character flaws that make the rest of us cringe. This type of behavior is unacceptable, and we don't want to expose ourselves to the demands of this world when we're not at our best. It is no wonder that so many of us would rather deny our pain and sorrow than go through it.

When we deny a situation, we cover up the pain and act as if everything is normal. Yet we must feel the pain in order to begin to heal. When we refuse to feel the pain, we also numb ourselves from other emotions such as love, joy, laughter, which make life bearable and enjoyable. You need to feel all emotions, whether negative or positive, in order to quickly get on the road to healing from your loss. When a person's denial becomes so acute that he or she refuses to face life as it is, or does not want to live the new reality, a therapist is needed. Only a professional can really assist someone in this disconnected state.

Bargaining

It is common to begin to bargain prior to a loved one's death, asking God to please spare his life in return for a changed behavior of some sort. *I will give up smoking,* or *I will go to church from now on.* Bargaining occurs right after a loss as well. It is a phase we use as a way to control a situation. Bargaining is another type of defense mechanism. I have worked with people who are so deeply in shock and denial about a death that they actually go on living their lives as though nothing has happened. They live in a suspended reality. One woman continued to make her husband's dinner night after night, thinking that he would be coming home to eat it. She even talked to him as though he were in the room with her. This conversation would continue every day. Another woman kept waiting for her dead child to walk through the door. Every time the phone or doorbell rang, she ran to answer it, expecting it to be her child. She thought that maybe there had been a mistaken identity, and her child would return any day. In her mind she thought that God would give her child a second chance at life.

Bargaining is quite common when a person is not present at the time of death, or is away during the funeral. In these instances, one does not see the death with his or her own eyes, and therefore continues to believe that it did not really happen. He or she never said good-bye.

Bargaining is also used in situations such as divorce or being laid off from a job. A person makes a promise to God that if he or she behaves a particular way, then everything will be reversed, or the scenario will be prevented by some miraculous occurrence. Despite the cruel reality, though, time cannot be turned back. Bargaining, like denial, keeps us from facing reality. Many people believe that a miracle will happen, and they try to bargain with God in the hope that by turning over a new leaf, the situation will return to normal. Sometimes the shock of loss can become too much to bear, and we resort to this kind of reasoning.

Bargaining temporarily comforts some people as they ease into the truth of the situation. This stage of grief and loss is normal to a certain point, but if it continues too long, it can deter your healing and your ability to move on with your life. I know some people who go in and out of this stage for years. However, if you live in an illusionary world where denial and bargaining are totally encompassing, you begin to detach from the reality around you. One must be an active participant in life on all levels—physically, mentally, emotionally, and spiritually.

Anger

Try to remember the last time you were in a situation in which you felt that no matter what you did, you couldn't get out of it. Did you feel powerless? Or was there a sense that it was out of your control and that there was some other force involved? The sense of being powerless and out of control are characteristics of feeling angry. It is very common to be angry when someone dies because death is the one event that we cannot control.

First of all, your anger is directed at those who you feel are responsible for placing you in your particular situation. You are angry at the deceased for leaving you to fend for yourself. A husband or wife is angry at each other for causing a divorce.

You are angry at the boss who has just fired you. You say to yourself, *How could you do this to me?* Second, you blame God for the untimely situation. You feel victimized by some unseen power that wants to punish you. *How could God rob this life from me, or place me in this horrible situation?* Finally, you are angry with yourself. *I could have done something to keep her alive. I should have known better. How could I have gotten myself into this awful situation?*

In my work I have often dealt with people who were very angry over the death of a loved one. Often they feel abandoned. *He left me with a mess. She had no right to leave me alone.* Some of the anger is due to financial difficulties, particularly if the deceased was in charge of the money. Some anger is aimed at doctors or the hospital staff for not taking better care of the deceased when he or she was alive. Some are angry with themselves for not being good enough to their loved ones. *I didn't tell her I loved her enough. I complained too much when he was alive.* A survivor may display this anger in many ways, such as temper tantrums or outbursts. Or the anger can be turned inward against oneself, creating depression or despair.

Some people stay in a state of anger for extended periods, and some tend to be angry for the rest of their life. It is okay to feel angry for a while. In fact, it is quite normal. Even though it is not pleasant to feel this way, it is part of the process. We have a right to be upset. We have to be able to express ourselves, so expressing anger is healthy. So often people feel they shouldn't be angry and repress their feelings of powerlessness. As long as we repress or keep down our unexpressed anger, the longer it stays inside our bodies. Usually, it will surface in the body as disease or some form of disability. You must remember that the body will only produce what is fed into it. If you store resentment and anger, they can also show up in other areas of your life. They may affect your relationships with others. They may diminish your capacity to work efficiently and achieve success. You may get depressed a lot, so you start to take some sort of drugs to feel better. One day you wake up and don't understand why your life is such a mess. If you are able to trace back your feelings, you may find that you have never expressed your anger for a situation in which you felt out of control. You have never let your anger out.

Anger is the one emotion that is definitely evident in a person's interactions with other people. We can feel someone's anger intuitively. I see it in my work all the time. Sometimes a person will yell at someone or will scream for no apparent reason. He or she is not even aware that such an outburst is really covering up deeply rooted pain. The more a person bottles up her feelings, the more likely she is set to explode. This could lead to devastating consequences. This is true especially for teens whose friends die untimely deaths. If they are not equipped to deal with their anger, they may express it violently. That is why it is so important to allow everyone, including children and teens, to talk about their feelings. Unexpressed grief in teens, especially in males, can lead to deadly massacres and gang violence.

It would be better if we all learned to let out our anger without hurting others. There are many safe ways to express anger. Physical exertion and activity is one way to help move this type of energy out of the body. If you are angry at someone, it's okay to tell them without "going ballistic." It's also okay to go off somewhere and scream. I tend to let off steam in the privacy of my own room. We must vent our anger; otherwise it will turn into rage. And we all know how rage is acted out in our society. When our anger is released, we feel relieved. We got it "off our chest."

If you are on the receiving end of a verbal attack or alienation, you must realize that an individual is in some sort of pain. You are merely helping him or her to let off steam. Dealing with someone else's anger can be intimidating to most of us, especially if we don't know how to handle our own feelings of inner conflict. Remember that you don't need to defend yourself. If you retaliate against another, you just escalate the other person's aggression into more anger. My favorite way to handle feelings of anger when someone provokes me is to count slowly to ten. I find that it lessens the emotional energy that I am feeling and allows me the time to take control of my thoughts and feelings once again.

Guilt

Another very common reaction to loss is guilt. Most people do not realize that guilt is a genuine phase of grieving. Often people will feel as though they have failed in a duty or an obligation, or that they have done something wrong. Another aspect of guilt is self-blame. For instance, when a mother and father lose a child, they frequently feel as though they were responsible for the child's death. This might be unrealistic but true nevertheless. The parents become overwrought with guilt. I once did two readings back to back at a conference in Phoenix, Arizona, and both cases involved the death of a child. The first was a girl killed in a car accident, and the second was a boy on a motorcycle hit by a car. In both instances the fathers felt guilty for the death. They felt they should have warned their children somehow, or kept them out of harm's way. Because parents are a child's protectors, when a child dies, they automatically feel as though they did not do a good enough job. These two parents really believed that they were at fault. When the spirits of their children came through, they told their fathers that there was nothing that they could have said or done to stop the accidents from happening. "You couldn't warn me enough about the accident," said the girl to her father. "It was something I had to go through, and there was nothing you could do to prevent it." In addition, parents always feel they should die first. It's logical, of course, but we have to keep in mind that we are on a spiritual journey. Life is not limited to the material world. Even so, a child's death always feels like a personal failure to a parent. Their guilt usually turns into feelings of worthlessness and condemnation.

Guilt is even more profound when you are part of the tragedy that took someone's life. This is known as "survivor's guilt." For instance, someone you love died in a car accident while you were at the wheel. When people are involved in any type of disaster, like plane crashes, shootings, bombings, etc., the grief of the survivors is enormous. They damn themselves. *Why didn't I sit in that seat? I lived a long life, why didn't I go instead? She was a good person. It should have been me.* Survivors feel guilty because they are alive while someone else passed away. There is the added pressure from members of the deceased's family who will tend to secretly blame the survivors for surviving.

Often when loved ones die, many issues are left unresolved. We wish we could have told the person how sorry we were for something we said or did in the past. We feel guilty that we didn't keep our promises. We should have made some sort of reconciliation beforehand. We rack our brains with *if only this* or *if only that.* Many times we feel guilty over insignificant details. *He always loved chocolate ice cream. Why didn't I get it for him more often?* We somehow equate the chocolate ice cream with prolonging life or perhaps making the end more bearable. We must be careful not to manipulate our thoughts into guilt. That is why we must have a clear understanding of the reasons behind our thoughts.

Many times people feel guilty because they were not present when a loved one passed over. This comes up a lot in my readings. Most of the time a spirit chooses to leave when no one is around anyway. It is rare, if ever, that spirits blame others for not being with them at the end. Death is always a choice, not an accident waiting to happen. There is no need to burden ourselves with guilt about this.

People also feel guilty about feeling happy or relieved about a situation. *I shouldn't be this happy. This shouldn't happen to me; I am not worthy of it.* These self-criticisms and doubts always impair our self-image and have long-lasting and damaging effects throughout our lifetime.

Blaming ourselves for a death or any other dreadful situation that occurs in our lives is common. We wring our hands and pull our hair. We curse our shortcomings and repeat our "should-haves." We feel guilty because we think that by doing so, something will change. Perhaps if we can rationalize why a person died, or why we lost the house, or why we got cancer, we can create reasons for putting the blame on ourselves. Then we can punish ourselves for something we feel we could have prevented. This is the trouble with guilt.

In all these circumstances, we need to properly and honestly evaluate our situations, and see if we are creating unrealistic scenarios and feeding more into them than exists. Can we move on? Is it time to let go of a relationship or situation in our lives? We must decide without prejudice or blame. Feeling guilty over something that has passed will not change it. Having guilt will certainly hamper your progress in healing your heart. Instead, try to look at the situation objectively for what it is. Ask yourself, *What lesson am I learning from this? How will it change my life? Will I be a more compassionate and loving person because of it?* In the end, ask yourself if this newly discovered knowledge would help someone else. If it can, then you are choosing to heal your life rather than wallow in guilt.

Sadness and Depression

Sadness is the emotion most apparent after a loss. We experience the depth of despair and the lowest of lows. We begin to close ourselves off from social interactions. We place ourselves in a self-imposed isolation where we feel all alone and totally helpless. We fall into a depression of sorts. This is one of the hardest stages to go through, and one that may last a considerable time. Often sadness and depression are undercurrents that run through the entire grieving process. We realize that the person we lost, whether it is a spouse, a relative, a friend, or a child, will no longer be with us physically. We know that we will never see our loved one again. We wonder, *How will I go on?* The same is also true when we lose a pet, our home or job, or someone close gets a terrible illness. Sadness and sorrow fill our hearts. We recognize that a situation has been changed, and life will never be the same way again. Whatever was comfortable and familiar is gone. It becomes difficult to go back home and begin living all alone, or to rearrange our lives to take care of an elderly parent. We wonder why life is so hard. We may feel as if we are drowning and no one is around to throw us a life preserver. We think about our own mortality, our own desires, and our future. *Does life have any real meaning? What are we here for?* We find ourselves feeling weary about many things, but have no way to change them. It is important that one recognize signs of depression and be able to honestly come to terms with what one is experiencing. Mild depression is normal during the grieving process. It means you are feeling and reacting to a loss.

Depression can take over our lives especially if we have no spiritual center inside ourselves. If we have no true spiritual understanding of the meaning of life and death, we will find ourselves struggling to come to terms with our loss. This is the time to develop our spiritual identities. At the back of the book you will find exercises and meditations that will help you to focus on the spirit within.

Depression becomes harmful when it lingers for too long. A person can walk around like a zombie, or become a recluse. Again, when any stage of grief becomes totally encompassing, our ability to function as active participants in life will stop. So, too, will our healing. One has to realize that unhealthy grieving is a retardant to the spirit. We must remember that we are still alive, and therefore we still have a purpose to fulfill. God makes no mistakes. The following are some of the symptoms of severe depression:

- Loss of interests that once were part of your life
- Drastic change in diet and sleep patterns
- Frequent and uncontrollable outbursts of crying
- The need to be totally alone
- Withdrawal from all social activities
- Feelings of absolute hopelessness and helplessness
- Thoughts of suicide

When we are in severe depression, getting help can be very difficult. That is why it is necessary to have a support person or group in our lives.

Physical Manifestations of Grief

Fear and anxiety are part of the grieving process also. Fear is something one doesn't expect to encounter, because sadness and sorrow fill so much of one's days. But we do become anxious and fearful of a future without our spouse or partner or friend. After the loss of a home or job, we may become afraid of the dark, or fearful of taking any type of risk. Life is like a mirror. It reflects back to us what we put into it. Constant fear and worry usually manifest in the body through a variety of physical symptoms and ailments such as these:

- Loss of appetite
- Dizziness and fainting
- Heart palpitations
- Loss of memory and concentration
- Insomnia
- Headaches
- Dry mouth
- Stomach cramps
- Elimination problems
- Sweaty palms
- Lack of daily hygiene
- Inability to swallow
- Muscular aches and pains

When we go through some sort of trauma in our lives, our bodies naturally react in a variety of ways. It is normal to feel apprehensive or anxious during the grieving process. We are uncertain and confused. We may even feel panicky. These feelings are all normal. We have been through a very difficult ordeal. One woman wanted a reading with me, but she could not leave her home after her husband's death. She had been married at the age of eighteen, and was separated only one day from her husband in thirty years of marriage. Her self-esteem was so closely tied to her husband that she felt she had lost her identity. Her role as wife, partner, and lover was over. "Who am I?" she asked. She became confused and disoriented and developed agoraphobia. She had difficulty sleeping and eating as well. She was too afraid to step outside, so she couldn't go back to work, and there was great financial strain placed on her family. These symptoms persisted for about a year as she grieved the loss of her beloved husband. Little by little, with the help of friends and her children, some of her confidence began to return, and her fear began to subside. Today, she has a new job and is doing much better.

It is important to realize that our physical symptoms are actually part of our emotional state. One cannot exist without the other. The butterflies in the stomach, the dry throat or mouth, insomnia, etc., are manifestations of the sadness, fear, guilt, and anxiousness one feels as part of his or her grief. If we have lost a child, we become anxious for our other children's welfare. If we have lost a job, we become fearful that we might become homeless, or worse, that we will be shunned by our friends and neighbors. These thoughts of doom and gloom are for the most part unrealistic, yet they seem real enough at the time.

As you express your feelings and process the various stages of grieving, you will begin to feel some relief. A good cry can help you work through your sadness and fear. Talking to friends and neighbors will help to ground yourself into reality. Remember that these feelings are temporary, and you are not going crazy.

Acceptance

Acceptance is the final goal of the grieving process. When we come to this stage, we are acknowledging the situation for what it is. We need to accept the loss so that we can heal our wounds and move on with our lives. It does not mean, however, that we necessarily find it agreeable, or that we are finished grieving. We are still experiencing stages of loss and grief, and we will fall back from time to time into depression, guilt, and the other feelings again. We go in and out of the grieving process. There are no set rules or time limits.

With acceptance one comes to the understanding that life is given to us with a certain amount of situations that we cannot control or change. At this point we can look at life, and the people and situations in it, in a new way. Hopefully, we have gained knowledge and wisdom for our own future in order to benefit ourselves and others. By accepting our loss, we have begun the process of resolution and restoration. We may reevaluate our lives and ask ourselves, *What has this situation taught me? What opportunities has it brought my way? How different am I now?*

At this stage we can reinvest in ourselves and our futures. We can proceed with the realization that our loved one has died, or the situation is over, and without diminishing the sadness or heartache we feel, we can turn our focus to living life. We may create an entirely new set of values for ourselves. We may decide to sell our house and move to a new location. We may decide to return to college or change our occupation. We may let go of friends and acquaintances that were negative or invalidating in their relationship with us. We may decide to volunteer at the grief-support group that has helped us in many ways. We may decide to take more walks or spend more time in nature. Whatever we decide, we will find that there are opportunities born out of our loss, and although life cannot return to what it once was, there are still things for us to do while we inhabit this classroom called earth.

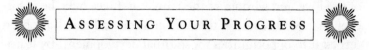

ASSESSING YOUR PROGRESS

During the grieving process your reactions to situations are magnified. Depending on many factors, like diet, sleep, work, stress, etc., you may feel out of control one moment and numb the next. There may be times when outside help is necessary. A friend, a neighbor, a relative, or a support group is extremely valuable. Remember that you will not get a new attitude overnight. Besides, it is important to create a support system to assist you during those times when things seem darkest. The more isolated you are, the more difficult the grieving, and the slower the healing process. If negative behavior dominates your behavior, professional help may be necessary. Unhealthy grieving emerges as excessive drinking or drug taking; chronic health problems like ulcers and headaches; compulsive behavior patterns like spending too much money, or overeating; violence; frequent nightmares; and constant thoughts of suicide. If these problems persist, please seek help from your local doctor, therapist, minister, rabbi, or priest. Most hospitals and churches can assist you in finding help through their grief-counseling services. Sometimes a group situation is extremely beneficial because you are able to learn from others going through the same torment. Also, there are a variety of websites now available for grief support, and I have listed various organizations at the end of the book for your information. We all need a little help to get us back on track.

As you read through the next part of the book, you will find that the grieving process varies with each individual situation. No matter where you are in your process, I hope that the healing words from my readings, which have been a source of comfort and renewal for many, will help you in your hour of need. The words of spirit confirm the continuation of life and speak

of the love and wisdom of the Universe. Lives have been forever changed because of them. Confusion and pain have been
turned into opportunities for spiritual development. By learning not to fear death, people have learned to enjoy life. Some
have even come to regard the passing of a loved one as a gift
from spirit in learning to overcome the illusion of control over
circumstances and events. Others have recognized that change
is inevitable and have learned to accept it and create new interests in their lives.

When we can tap into that God Force energy within ourselves, we are able to help others help themselves. That is
what I hope to convey through the evidential material presented in the next part of the book. As you process your grief,
you will continue to change and grow on a personal level.
Everything is always a choice, and the choice is always yours to
make. Through my communication with the other side of life,
I, too, am continually learning from spirit about the necessity
of choosing love and forgiveness for myself and for all people.

The Dash

I read of a man who stood to speak
at the funeral of a friend.
He referred to the dates on her tombstone
From the beginning—to the end.

He noted that first came the date of her birth
And spoke of the following date with tears
But he said what mattered most of all
· Was the dash between those years.

For the dash represents all the time
That she spent alive on earth . . .
And now only those who loved her
Know what that little line is worth.

For it matters not how much we own:
The cars . . . the house . . . the cash.
What matters is how we live and love
And how we spend our dash.

So think about this long and hard . . .
Are there things you'd like to change?
For you never know how much time is left,
(You could be at "dash mid-range.")

If we could just slow down enough
To consider what's true and real,
And always try to understand
The way other people feel.

And be less quick to anger,
And show appreciation more
And love the people in our lives
Like we've never loved before.

If we treat each other with respect,
And more often wear a smile . . .
Remembering that this special dash
Might only last a little while.

So, when your eulogy's being read
With your life actions to rehash . . .
Would you be proud of the things they say
About how you spent your dash?

—*Linda M. Ellis*

PART II

When Someone You Love Dies

3

A DEATH IN
THE FAMILY

*W*hen a parent dies, a part of ourselves dies also. We are devastated. Much of what we feel at first is confusion and uncertainty as the security blanket we labeled "parent" is gone, and we are truly left on our own. A parent's death is a disturbing event for many reasons, but especially because it reminds us of our own mortality as physical beings.

Depending upon the dynamics of the family, whether it was ideal or not, when a parent dies, we also mourn for our lost selves— our lost childhood. Parents are the very first humans to touch our lives, and as such they are the first ones who teach us about the ways of the world. They are in fact our very

first loves. As infants we rely on them for all our needs and desires and feel protected in the comfort of their caresses. They
are our shields of safety against the negative influences of the
unknown existence around us. For many they are our biggest
fans, forever encouraging us to do our best even when we feel
our worst. Our parents are usually the only ones we can count
on when life is overwhelming or unkind. Therefore, much of
our world is built through the eyes and minds of our parents,
and as much as we would like to deny it, there are aspects of
our parents deeply ingrained in us. We identify ourselves with
our parents. That is why when we lose a parent, we are confused and unsettled, as if we were standing naked on an unfamiliar highway. We are at a crossroads, and we don't have a
clue about which way to go. Our protection, our home, our
sanctuary is gone, and we are forever changed.

While a parent is still alive, we often dismiss the idea of his
or her dying as something way off in the future, not really giving it too much thought. Subconsciously, we think of our parents as immortal, as if they were some sort of gods. Or we figure
that as one gets old, it's only natural to die, as that is nature's
way of recycling. We rationalize to ourselves that at the time it
happens, we will be ready for it. But are we ever? As you will
read from my own personal experience, no matter what the
circumstances are, we are never ready to face the death of a
parent.

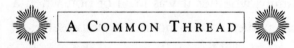

A COMMON THREAD

Many of the readings I have done over the years have involved a parent's passing. The feelings, reactions, and stages of
grief vary in degree with each situation, but an undeniable

commonality exists among those whose parents have died. Generally, there are several unresolved emotional issues that surface. Most involve situations a person may have kept hidden since childhood. For instance, after the death of a parent, it is quite common to experience a certain amount of guilt. This guilt could involve one or all of the following examples:

I could have told Dad I loved him.
Why didn't I tell Mom I was sorry when she was alive?
Why didn't I visit or call Mom more often?
If I paid more attention, I could have done something to prevent his death.

As we will learn from the second reading in this section, some of us live our entire lives in our parents' shadow. Many are left feeling bitter and lonely, and sometimes desperate. They cry, *How could you leave me?* Some nurse a sick parent for many years, and when that parent is gone, they are afraid to get on with life. They fall into a depression and can't seem to pick themselves up and make a new start.

Blame is another very common emotion that surfaces after a parent's death. We blame anyone and everyone, from the doctor, to a sibling, to a surviving parent. We feel powerless, so we lash out and blame something or someone for taking our parent away. We may be adult in age, but we feel like a child inside. *If only you hadn't done this or that. Why did you say that? You should have . . . or you could have.*

It is also a time when we feel angry, cheated, and resentful. We may be angry at ourselves, our dead parent, or the world in general. We might remember a traumatic experience with a parent such as abuse or abandonment. *Why did you do that to me? I hate you. You ruined my life. I am happy you are dead.* We have to find a way of venting anger that is safe for ourselves and others. Here again, it may be best to seek some therapeutic assistance through a support group or a counselor.

On the other hand, there are many parents who were our best friends, confidantes, and sounding boards, as the third reading illustrates. Losing them is like losing our right arms. We feel abandoned, sad, lonely, and depressed. *Who will I talk to about my problems? Who will listen to me? No one can give me that special kind of caring and love.* When such a strong bond of attachment is severed, a person may weep a lot and feel sorry for herself, or she may want to retreat from life. Sometimes the sadness is so deep and overwhelming, a person becomes physically ill.

As I said, the death of a parent may lead us to a juncture in our lives. Standing at that crossroads, we must begin to ask ourselves: *What have I learned from Mom or Dad? Do I want to live my life in a different way now that he or she is gone? What do I really want out of life?* You may need to finally forgive a parent for the way he or she treated you. Maybe it's time for you to say *I'm sorry* to your parent. Perhaps it is an opportunity for you to get closer to other family members and rise above any differences you may have had with them. Or you may become aware of a particular aspect of yourself that you have not explored while your parent was alive. Maybe your parent's death will force you to see the world in a different and more beneficial manner.

Even though the parental structure has been broken, and at times you feel devastated, you will get through it. That is part of the process of grieving. It just might be the perfect time for you to make an important choice that will lead to a new life's direction.

Most of us will experience the deaths of both our parents in our lifetimes, and although we all share a common bond of feeling hurt, sad, or lonely as we mourn, the healing process is never quite the same for each. My desire is that all of us children left behind will understand that our parents will always remain alive within us.

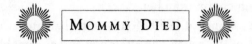

MOMMY DIED

My mother and I had a very special relationship. I was the youngest of four children, and I was always reminding her how the youngest in the family got the short end of the stick. I would often tell her that by the time I was born, there were only leftovers—toys, clothes, and even affection. This wasn't true, but I would do anything to get her attention. Throughout my childhood my mother was my Rock of Gibraltar. So was my father, but in a different way. He was always working, and I thought of him more as the provider and backbone of the family.

My earliest memories of Mom were the times when she would walk me to nursery school. I would hold her hand and tell her that I didn't want to leave her because I missed being with her during the day. I told her that the other kids were not as fun as she was. She would just laugh and squeeze my hand. As a youngster I was quite small, and the bigger boys would constantly tease me. She would say, "Let me know who is picking on you, and I will give him the back of my hand." I always loved that expression of hers. It was a reminder of her Irish heritage and fiery temper. From a very early age, I have always viewed my mother as my playmate and protector.

Nowadays, when people see me in person at a demonstration, a book signing, or even a social event, they are surprised at my sense of humor. They tell me how appreciative they are of my laughter. I tell them that my humor is a gift from my mother. She had an incredible wit and a tremendous laugh that was completely contagious. She had a way of making everyone smile, especially when she spoke with her fake Irish brogue. The twinkle in her eye was as mischievous as that of a leprechaun's. I am happy to say I inherited a little bit of that leprechaun charm from her.

In the summer of 1980 Mom's sunny laughter stopped. She sat down on the couch one afternoon and was unable to speak or move her arms. My siblings and I immediately called our father at his job. He told us to get Mom to the hospital, and we called the paramedics who brought her to the emergency room. We all sat in the waiting room until early the next morning as the doctors put Mom through a battery of tests. Finally, we were given the results. Mom had had a major stroke that left her right side paralyzed and her verbal ability completely impaired. The woman who could light up a room with her smile was forever silenced.

It struck us all very hard. We spent the next several days cross-examining doctors and specialists for more information. *Will she ever talk again? What are her chances of walking? How much longer does she have to live?* No one could provide us with answers, or at least the answers we wanted to hear. Days soon turned into weeks, and my mother recovered only slightly. After two months she managed to walk a bit, move her right hand, and blink her eyes. For anyone who has experienced a stroke or knows someone who has, it is painful to watch a strong and vital person become completely immobile. I felt so helpless, as did the rest of the family. None of us were ever quite sure of what to do. One of my first reactions was to blame God for her affliction. She was such a devoted Catholic; she would walk a mile to church every morning. *Why would God do this to someone so devoted and loving? Maybe God made a mistake.*

Two years after my mother's stroke, I moved to Los Angeles to start a career. I began working as a temp for Embassy television. Norman Lear was head of production and was creating such shows as *All in the Family*, *One Day at a Time*, and *Sanford and Son*—all huge hits on TV. When I heard about a permanent position at the Los Angeles office of People for the American Way, a nonprofit organization formed by Lear and others, I jumped at the opportunity. At the time I wanted to break into television as a writer, and I thought getting this job was one step closer to fulfilling my dream. How wrong I was. Little did I know that my assignment had nothing to do with television production. I was a representative's assistant, and my position consisted of opening mail, recording donations, and preparing for guest events. Like most assistants, I spent the day running errands to the post office and bank and returning with everyone's lunch. Actually, I liked my job a lot, and when I look back at that time, I realize that it taught me an invaluable lesson. When I first started the job, I had no idea what the organization was about. As I sorted through the mail every day, I became aware that the aim of People for the American Way was to fight the spread of ignorance and prejudice. As I read through the contents of the letters sent to the office, I realized that there were a lot of hateful people who used religion as a tool for their particular cause. Millions of letters containing fearful propaganda were sent to ordinary citizens, condemning abortion as murder, referring to homosexuality as demonic, and demanding that the Bible be taught in public schools. To me it was pure fascism palming itself off as Americanism, and I applauded the efforts of this group and liked my job all the more.

During my days in the office, I would often find myself daydreaming of my family back East. I had left them some time ago and fought a constant inner battle of whether to continue living in Los Angeles and struggle to be a TV writer, or chuck it all and find a job back home in New York. It was difficult when a birthday rolled around and I wasn't there to celebrate with a niece or nephew. I knew that they were growing older, and I wasn't part of their lives. *Would they even know Uncle Jamie when they met me?* The only time I ever saw them was at Christmas, when I would make a yearly pilgrimage to reunite with all my relatives. Not one day went by when I didn't find myself thinking about my family. It was especially difficult because my mother was so ill. To this day, I often think that maybe if I lived back East I could have done something to save her.

It was on one of these Christmas reunions with my family, two years after I had moved to California, that I saw Mom for the last time. By this time we had full-time care for her in one of New York's finest nursing facilities. My brother Michael and my dad had just brought her back to the nursing home after our Christmas feast. I had to say good-bye to her, as I was returning to L.A. on the afternoon flight. I looked into her eyes, that beautiful sea of crystal blue, and she gazed back at me, trying her best to tell me something. Unfortunately, I understood all too well, and I excused myself and left the room. I sat in the hallway and cried my eyes out. I knew at that moment that it was the last time I would ever see my mother alive again. I felt her pain and knew that she was tired of carrying around her withered body. It must have been so frustrating for someone so demonstrative to suddenly come to a complete halt. I knew that she wanted no more of this life. I barely remember the airplane ride back to Los Angeles. However, I do remember that from that moment on, I asked everyone in the spirit world to assist her in making her passing quick and painless. I hoped with all my heart that they could hear me and help in some way.

I'll never forget that fateful day the rest of my life. It was Tuesday, February 28, and I awakened with a strange, unsettling feeling in my stomach. At 12:30 P.M., I received a phone call from my sister Lynn. I still can hear her voice shrieking, "Jamie, Mommy died." I thought I was prepared for that moment. After all, I knew my mother was ready to die. I prayed constantly that when her time came, the spirit world would ease her pain. Yet when I heard the word "died," my reaction was something I *never* expected. I was in total shock. I managed to say something to my supervisor, who put her arms around me in a comforting gesture. I left the office in a fog and still do not know how I arrived at the Catholic church five blocks away. I lit a candle for Mom and prayed for her peaceful transition. I somehow managed to go home and pack a bag for my trip to New York.

At the funeral I was visibly upset. I listened to the priest on the pulpit eulogize my mother and thought, *He must be talking about someone else. How can she be gone?* That whole day remains a clouded memory. I can't recall how I got from one place to another, to whom I talked, or even what I did. I felt alone among the crowd of people. It was so hard to believe that my mother was not in the midst of everyone, telling her jokes, making them laugh, and giving me a wink. Everything was a blur that day. Not only was I in a state of shock, but also in a state of denial.

At this time I had just begun to contact the spirit world on my own. Four months after my mother's death, my new friend and teacher, medium Brian E. Hurst, asked if I wanted to speak with her on the other side. Even though I knew I could never have her back physically, I was extremely encouraged to know that she was alive in another form and comforted by the fact that she was watching over me from heaven.

People often ask me, "Can you read for yourself?" No, I re-

ally can't. Let me qualify that. I am aware of a loved one's spirit
in the room, but I am too emotionally attached to the situation to know whether it is my own desire to hear something or
my own emotions getting in the way of a spirit's message. In
other words, it is very difficult to know if I am creating what
my mother is saying because I want her to say something in
particular, or if she is indeed giving me her own distinct message.

I arrived at Brian's home with my father, who was visiting
me at the time. We couldn't wait for the séance to begin. I sat
with anticipation at the opportunity to hear my mother speak
through the voice of an independent medium who knew nothing about her. Brian closed his eyes, said a prayer, and began.

"I have a spirit here," he started. But it was not my mother.
Instead it was my father's mother. Brian gave Dad some very
good evidence about the street she lived on and the subway
she used to take to work. Then suddenly he exclaimed,

"Jean, I hear a lady saying Jean is here."

It was Mom! I was so excited, I could barely breathe. I
didn't know how to feel. Part of me couldn't believe it, and the
other part of me was overjoyed.

"She is here with her sisters Mary and Betty," said Brian.

"Yes, those are her sisters," I responded. I was so happy. My
mother was in the room, and we could all feel her presence so
clearly. Dad was completely dumbfounded.

"Jamie, she is calling you Jamie," Brian continued.

"Yes, I understand that," I said.

"Your mother has a wonderful laugh, and everyone knows
that laugh. She has made many people laugh over there."

I could hardly believe what he was saying. Yes, indeed it was
the lady who could make a joke out of anything and could
keep people in stitches for hours at a time.

Then Brian began to cry. He assured me that he was okay. "Your mother wants to thank you for praying for her, James. She says it helped a great deal. She wants you to know she is able to walk and talk again. She is very funny . . . she is telling me that she can't keep her mouth shut!"

Bingo! How relieved I was to know she was completely whole again, and the same person I knew and loved.

Then Brian got quiet. "Jean is telling me that a priest came to meet her. It was a Catholic priest she knew earlier in her life. A Father James Reilly."

My father couldn't believe it. He was obviously blown away by the information. He screamed out, "That's the old priest she knew when I first met her. Oh, my God, that's amazing!"

The reading continued as Brian accurately relayed details about my mother's life and that of my father's. At the end of the session, Brian looked at me with a blank expression and said something that has remained with me to this day.

"James, your mother wants me to tell you that one day you will be very well known, and you will help a lot of people."

I wasn't quite sure what to make of this last comment. I thought she meant I would become a famous TV writer like Norman Lear, and perhaps help people through an organization like his. I had no idea that she meant I would help others as a medium.

"Your mother wants you to know that she is a guide of yours."

I felt very relieved by this last remark of Brian's.

He continued, "She wants me to tell you that she is still your protector and always will be."

The only way to describe the sensations I felt is to say it was like someone gently patting my heart. Nothing more needed to be said. I knew I had my mom forever.

An Individual Process

No one is ever prepared for the death of a parent. We may think we are, but we are not. What I went through when my mother died is quite common. After the numbness and denial, I remember being mad at God, because "He" caused it. However, as I reflect back, I see that my mother's death was an incredible opportunity for me. I realized that the ending of a physical life is not the ending of life. The grief that I felt at her passing was very real and very emotionally draining, but I was able to gather my strength back little by little, day by day. In time the pain subsided, and I began to heal.

There are no rules about the grieving process because each one of us deals with loss in a different way. There is the saying, however: *When one door closes, another one opens.* If we can look at death in this way, as a door closing, we can find comfort in knowing that a new door is about to open.

I have been a medium for many years and have touched the spirit world practically on a daily basis. Every time I read for an individual, I am still amazed at how that initial communication, or opening the door to spirit, changes a person's life forever. The fear of death is vanished, and life takes on a whole new meaning. Most people will never have an opportunity to sit with a medium, or be able to see or hear the spirit world. But that's not necessary to become aware of one's own spirituality. Many of us can use prayer or meditation to open ourselves to our spiritual side. Remember that spirituality is our birthright. It is who we are first and foremost. Hard as it may be to understand completely, we live in a physical body in a physical world as spiritual beings. When we realize the *spiritualness* of who we are, we will find a great support system all around us.

Grieving is a great opportunity to grow, to understand, and to explore ourselves. Tears clean the windows of our souls. Sometimes we think our heart is broken beyond repair, but perhaps we can see it as broken so it can let in more of our own light. The lesson of death is not one of blame or guilt or anger, but of love. The door closes so another one can open. We can use grief as a spiritual tool to find meaning, joy, and productiveness in our own lives.

I have included several cases in which people have done just that. They have taken the situation of a loved one's death and become more useful and alive because of it. I am always in awe of the courage, faith, and strength people have in a time of utter sorrow. How much greater they are having gone through the fires of the human heart only to come out of them with a clearer understanding of life.

Does the hurt ever get better? That's up to each individual. Sometimes the hurt propels us to grow so we don't become enslaved by it. I ask each individual to make the decision, as I once did, to see death as an opening to a higher life. If I just wallowed in the loss of my mother, I might never have explored the spiritual dimensions. I would not have been able to help so many people heal their own pain when a loved one dies. The kingdom of heaven is available to everyone. As a great master once said: *Knock and the door will be opened to you.*

PEGGY'S MOM

The following reading was most disturbing to me at the time. The sitter had a lot of self-loathing, anger, guilt, and bitterness. I didn't want to include it at first because I thought it was negative, but the participant asked me to include it since it was a turning point in her self-development and healing. She felt it would help others who suffer from similar circumstances, and I agreed.

I met Peggy at one of my workshops, which her friend Natalie had persuaded her to attend. We were midway through the readings when I looked out at the crowd and saw a white-haired spirit woman standing behind a rather oversized lady. The spirit woman looked a bit disheveled and placed her hands on the woman's shoulders, shaking her head from side to side.

I could not help but be drawn to the seated woman, and I asked, "May I work with you and communicate a message from spirit?"

She looked back with a startled expression. "Me? You want to talk to me?"

I nodded my head yes, and her friend encouraged her to stand up. Remember, I knew nothing of this lady before this day. Cautiously she stood with her head bowed down toward the ground. The spirit standing behind her had moved to the side and was glaring at me. I felt as if I had done something wrong.

"There is a woman standing next to you about five foot seven inches tall. She has white hair pulled straight back and is wearing a pair of glasses on a string around her neck. She is standing on your right side, which tells me she is your mother or from your mother's side of the family. Do you understand this?" I asked.

Slowly the woman raised her head and in a whisper replied, "Yes, I think so."

I asked her to hold the microphone closer to her mouth as I waited to receive mental thoughts and visions from the harsh-looking spirit next to her.

"Do you understand the name of Addie or Adelaide?"

"Yes, that is my mother."

"Your mother screamed a lot, didn't she? She is shouting in my ear right now. I am sending her thoughts, telling her that I can hear her, and telling her not to shout. Are you a teacher?" I asked.

Sheepishly she replied, "Yes, I am."

"Was your mother a teacher, too?"

"Yes, well, part-time. She really wanted me to be the full-time teacher."

"I don't mean to seem rude, but your mother is very abrupt with me. She really is used to getting her own way, isn't she?" I looked at the woman and knew she understood me completely.

I then began to see in my mind's eye some startling visions. I saw Peggy being beaten as a young child. I understood all too quickly, so I asked her to see me afterward for a private reading.

Many times when I am interviewed, I have been asked, "Why don't spirits ever come through who are living in hell?" These questions are usually based on a biblical interpretation of hell as a literal place of eternal damnation. I find this interpretation of hell used mostly to control people out of fear, and this fear has been subconsciously ingrained in our minds. In my experience as a medium, hell does not exist as an actual place, but is a state of consciousness. A spirit that inhabits this consciousness is constantly being tormented with thoughts and feelings of how he or she mistreated others on earth. The degree to which a person hurts another is the degree to which it inhabits a hellish state of consciousness. Spirits of like-mindedness gravitate together in the spirit dimensions, and that in itself can be quite a hell.

I could tell that Peggy's domineering mother was at a point where she still held on to her earthly mind-set. She was still trying to control her daughter from the spiritual side.

Alone with Peggy, I continued the reading.

"Your mother is telling me you didn't know any better, that you were stupid," I told her.

With tears in her eyes Peggy looked at me. "She always called me stupid. Mother was the smart one. She said that I took after my father's side of the family."

My heart went out to this poor woman who had no sense of her own self-worth.

"Your mom is talking about a pail. The pail has water in it. Now I am shown three o'clock. Your mother is talking about a towel?" I didn't know what it all meant, but I could see by the redness in Peggy's face that she did.

"She keeps on saying you're not doing it right. Where is the dinner? She is talking about burning dinner. She blames you for burning the dinner. Is that right?"

Peggy sucked in her lips, looked down at the floor, and nodded her head up and down.

"She is also speaking about the books. She is getting louder. You can't do it right, the books are out of order, she says."

By now Peggy's chin was quivering, and tears were rolling down her face. She wanted to say something but couldn't get it out. I waited a few moments and had started again when suddenly Peggy let out an extremely loud wail.

"*Goddamn her* . . . How could she? I tried my best, but it was never good enough. Goddamn you, Mother!"

Peggy's head shot upward toward the ceiling, and she continued.

"How could you leave me? I did what you wanted. I brought you to the doctor. I cleaned you. I cleaned the house. What was it I did wrong?"

Peggy became more and more outraged at her mother. It was obvious that she had been holding back her feelings for a very long time. I rarely encounter such volatile situations in a reading, but I knew Peggy had to let it out, so I encouraged her, reminding her that it was healthy to express her feelings.

After several minutes, when she seemed exhausted, I held Peggy and told her, "Everything is going to be all right. It's over. You don't have to deal with it anymore. It's time to say good-bye to all those horrendous memories of your mother. You are your own incredible person. You don't need to measure yourself by somebody else's view of you."

I sat with Peggy for some time talking about what she had just experienced. She said that all the things I was bringing through reminded her of the terrible life she had with her mother.

"I was the perfect daughter. I did everything my mother told me. My father left us when I was seven, and I always thought it was my fault. After that I made sure to do everything Mother always wanted. My mother never really liked going out of the house, but she had to work occasionally. She was always telling me how hard she worked, and I felt guilty that she had to work on account of me. I had to bathe her every afternoon at three o'clock, and if I was one minute late she would begin to holler. She also made me cook dinner because she was always lying down. Then she would tell me I burned her dinner on purpose. I remember wanting to take tap dancing classes, but Mother refused. She was afraid I would twist my ankle, and then I couldn't do the work around the house."

Peggy never married. "Mom always told me that men are not to be trusted. She never got over my father's rejection."

Peggy's mother had died the year before of a heart attack, and Peggy had not allowed herself to feel and grieve the death. She just became a robot, doing what her mother had programmed her to do. She had kept all the hurt and rage and resentment buried deep down inside her.

At one point Peggy asked her mother, "Why didn't you love me?"

Her mother replied, "Because your father loved you more than me!"

I invited Peggy's friend Natalie into the room, and together the three of us discussed Peggy's future and what her options might be. I persuaded Peggy to continue to have conversations with her mother by writing letters or writing down her thoughts and emotions in a journal. It takes a while before all the sensations and judgments are released, especially if a bad memory triggers some painful feelings.

When we identify too strongly with a parent, as Peggy had, we have very little sense of self. We become programmed to please others and think of ourselves least of all. This leads to a lack of self-respect and self-worth. Peggy's situation shows how deeply attached we can be to our parents even if they aren't the most loving and kindest of people. After all, we have grown familiar with their behavior, and as we all know, familiarity is comfortable. The family dynamic can range from loving and nurturing to cruel and cold and everything else in between. Our parents teach us what they have been taught, and if it is negative, that cycle continues from one generation to the next until somebody recognizes the descending spiral and makes changes to break the pattern. Sometimes circumstances become so harsh that we are forced to break the cycle of negative impulses and conditioning when it is most difficult, and that can be at a parent's death.

Unhealthy patterns must be recognized before we can change our lives. The desire to change leads to mixed-up thoughts and feelings because we don't know how to behave anymore. If our childhood was filled with abuse, like Peggy's, we can feel a lot of loneliness, abandonment, hate, and resentment that can manifest in physical, mental, and emotional ways. However, it is through our pain that we can find a new understanding of ourselves as unique individuals with our own likes and dislikes and values. As Peggy had to learn, many of us may have to re-think and reinvent ourselves anew. I have found that the grief process is hardest for people who decide to make positive changes. They have to create different images for themselves. They really have to start fresh and learn how to act and react in ways that are unfamiliar to them.

At fifty-two years old, Peggy had so much hurt stored inside her that I knew she would need further help, and I advised her to see a therapist who I thought would be appropriate for her care. Peggy's reading was very difficult for me, but one that was definitely needed.

I walked the two friends to the door of the auditorium and gave them both hugs. Peggy told me she had prayed to God to help her. "I think my prayers are beginning to be answered," she said to me as she turned and walked away.

Grieving the death of a parent or anyone must be done in our own time, not someone else's preordained time. One of the first steps we must do to take control of our lives is to *say good-bye to our parent*. I can't emphasize this enough. When we take a few moments to say good-bye, it is important that we do it with *forgiveness* and *love*, not with resentment and anger. We must look at the situation honestly and recognize it for what it was. If there is anger, we must let it out first. Then we can come to a place of forgiveness. Forgiveness is the very first step on the road to healing.

UPDATE

My reading with Peggy occurred about seven years ago, and I am happy to report that since that day Peggy began to work with a therapist. As part of her grieving process, she started to study meditation and massage therapy. Subsequently, Peggy has sold her mother's house and has moved to Las Vegas with her husband of two years. She is presently a substitute teacher, a part-time real estate agent, and a Reiki master. Oh yes, she makes sure to save at least a couple of nights a week for tap-dancing classes.

My Best Friend

It doesn't matter how enlightened one is or how much experience one has had with death, when a parent dies, the feeling of loss never really leaves. There are constant reminders like songs, birthdays, favorite meals, and special places as the memory of a parent is indelibly imprinted in our hearts. So often we are told to get over a loved one's death that we wonder if something is wrong with us if we think of the person too much. It's okay to think about a parent and honor the memories of times spent together. When these thoughts arise, we can use them to celebrate our parent's life—how she sang a particular song, or how much he enjoyed a certain meal, or how we laughed at some situation together.

This next reading reminds me of just how much we can miss a parent. Wendy and her father had a close, loving relationship. As Wendy once told me, "He was truly my best friend. We worked together, traveled together, and enjoyed life to the fullest together." But when her father died, Wendy's life came to a sudden halt. All the laughing and fun ceased to be.

At a friend's urging, Wendy called my office for an appointment. She told me, "Life has no meaning. I feel so lost and alone." Wendy was skeptical about coming to see me, but she was desperate enough to find out if her father was indeed still around her, and that he was all right. In her words, "I remember knocking on your door thinking how silly I felt. I thought,

What am I doing here? There is no possible way this guy could actually communicate with the dead."

When Wendy arrived, she began to take pictures and mementos of her father out of her purse to show me. I immediately waved at her to stop. "Don't show me or tell me anything. Let me tell you."

After a short prayer, I began the reading.

"There is a man here who gives you a lot of love. He is standing on your left, so I believe it is your father. He is very happy you came here today. He says he is doing okay. He never thought life existed the way it does."

Wendy seemed relieved to hear this bit of information.

"He is showing me a patio. I am seeing him sitting outside on the patio with two dogs at his side."

Wendy chimed in, "Yes, that's right. We sat on the patio every morning and had our coffee."

I could see that Wendy was starting to believe she was actually communicating with her dad.

"Your father is showing me a bookcase or wall unit. He is telling me that he likes it very much. It fits perfectly in the room."

"I just installed a wall unit last week in my bedroom," exclaimed Wendy.

"I am now being shown a woman. There is some dark patch around her. I believe this woman has a tumor of some sort. I think he is referring to your mother."

Wendy nodded. "Yes, that's right. My mother was just diagnosed with cancer."

"Your father wants me to reassure you that she will be fine. He says not to worry about her. He is saying, 'She's a fighter, and she'll beat the cancer.'"

"There is someone else here with your father. He is singing a song." I began to hum the melody I was hearing.

Wendy sat back, her eyes wide open in amazement.

"Do you know someone called Peter? He is with your father, and he is singing to him."

I kept humming a song about Rio and asked, "Is this Peter associated with Rio de Janeiro?"

Wendy practically jumped out of her chair. "Yes, he is! It's Peter Allen, the songwriter. He had a big hit called 'When My Baby Goes to Rio.' My dad and he were best friends."

"Peter is saying that he was the first one to meet your father over there, and they pal around together like they used to."

"I'm happy to hear that!" Wendy exclaimed.

I continued with the messages from Wendy's father, telling her significant things about their relationship.

"Your father has a lot of love for you. He says that he loves you very much and will always be with you. If you ever need to talk to him, he will be there for you. You will never be alone."

By then Wendy had tears in her eyes.

I concluded the reading by thanking the spirit world as always for their assistance and guidance in bringing through their messages.

That session helped Wendy come to a new understanding that death was not the end of her relationship with her father and best friend. She left the office feeling uplifted and renewed. The lost little girl had been given a second chance at life.

UPDATE

My reading with Wendy was five years ago. I am happy to report that she has started to take charge of her life. She has begun her own business, and it is booming. She told me that she is traveling all over the world. She also let me know her mother indeed survived her bout with cancer and is on the road to recovery.

During our phone conversation she said, "James, you have changed my life forever. Not only do I have the fond memories of my dad, but I also have the wonderful knowledge that he taught me. He inspired me to live life to the fullest, and to go beyond my expectations, to reach for my dreams and always have fun. More important, he taught me the value of family and friends. I have learned by his example how to be there for those who need me, and bring happiness to those close to me. I have taken his advice. His lessons of love have given me happiness."

Wendy has used the death of her father as an opportunity to see life from a new perspective. As she said, "I now realize that I never really lost my dad. We just have a different type of relationship. I feel my father's presence in my heart and soul. He is with me all the time now. I am so grateful to you for leading me on the path back to life. I now know there is a heaven, and Dad is there, and someday we will be together again."

 GOOD-BYE, GRANDMA

Grandparents are a special breed. The majority of them are positive and cheering fans to their grandchildren. They don't see our faults and quirks like our parents do. Instead, grandparents seem to perfect the wonderful talent of looking the other way, and see us as brilliant and pure beings. Grandparents have often been labeled the spoilers of children because they dote on us and lavish us with so much love and attention, which usually comes in the form of favorite foods and gifts. We

believe grandparents behave this way because they can kiss
their grandchildren at the end of the day, and wave good-bye
as they drive away. It is true. A grandparent is not fully in-
vested in raising a child as a parent is. He and she do have a lot
more room for tolerance. I believe, too, that in the wisdom of
their years, grandparents have learned that love is the only
thing of importance.

Many individuals have never had an opportunity to experience the warm love and kindness of these folks. Their grandparents have already passed into spirit. All a person has heard
is what his parent or aunts and uncles repeat in tales from the
past. The only history of this relative is known through the
yellowed photographs in a scrapbook. There are no remembrances of a grandfather's joke and the warmth of a grandmother's embrace.

For those of us who were, and still are, lucky enough to
have our grandparents around, we will forever hold them in a
very special place in our hearts. They will always be our cham-
pions. I have worked with many individuals whose grandparents were their surrogate parents. In these cases, when a
grandparent actually raises a child, the attention and love a
child receives seems to be doubled. These grandparents feel as
though they have to overcompensate for an absent parent.
They want to make absolutely sure that a child feels loved.
Therefore, when the death of a grandparent occurs, it can be
am extremely difficult experience.

By the time I was born, three of my grandparents had
already died without my ever having known them. My one
surviving grandmother, Ethel Burrows Van Praagh, was my father's mother. My first memory of her is when she lived in a
one-bedroom apartment on Seventy-fourth Street in Jackson
Heights, New York. My father used to drop me off at her home

every now and then to spend a weekend. She and I became the very best of friends.

At the end of her street was a main subway stop for the number 7 IRT train. I must have been five or six years old when Grandma took me by the hand and walked me up to the platform to see all the trains pulling in and out of the station. I recall how excited I was, and how I used to scream with the whistle of a train as it came barreling down the tracks.

Because my grandmother's apartment was located on a main street, there was always the hustle and bustle of people rushing to and from the street-lined stores and subway station. The best part of the day was our afternoons. Grandma was originally from England, and she still kept the custom of having afternoon tea. So at four o'clock everything stopped except the whistling of her teakettle. These were special days for me. I would watch my grandmother sip her tea as I savored my hot chocolate. When we finished, Grandma moved over to her wooden chair next to the living room window. I would climb on her lap, and together we would look out and watch the world pass by our window. We would even wave to the pedestrians and would make up stories about where we thought a person was going or where he was coming from. Sometimes the people saw us looking at them, and they would come over and start talking to us. It was great fun. It was from that chair in front of the window that my first views of life were formed.

Grandma used to love to tell me stories about growing up in the countryside of England. She loved to travel and meet people. She would often say, "Traveling is the best education you can ever have." I used to listen and wonder about these far-off places that she described so vividly. I also recall that it was my grandmother who taught me about helping people. This is perhaps a simple example, but one that stands out in my mind. My grandmother kept a cup full of dimes and nickels in her cupboard. When I asked her why, she told me, "For those times when I look out the window and see people parking their cars, and they have no money for the meters. So I give it to them."

One of the fondest memories of my grandmother was the night my father dropped me off at her apartment before he went into Manhattan. I opened the door and right next to her tall wooden chair I saw a small wooden one for me. She said, "You needed your own chair. Now when we look out the window, you will have a better view." We would spend hours and hours in those chairs. She would create stories, and I discovered the world through her eyes. I still have that tiny wooden chair sitting by a window in my house.

I was fourteen years old when my grandmother died. With her death my childhood was gone forever. I will never forget that bleak Sunday morning when my mother walked into my room and said, "Grandma died during the night." At first I couldn't believe it. I was in shock. I spent the rest of the day by myself, not talking to anyone because I thought no one could ever understand the bond my grandmother and I shared. I was so upset and felt so alone, I didn't know what to do. So, I decided to write her a letter.

The day of the funeral, I drove with my father to the cemetery and stood at my grandmother's grave. In between my tears I read her the letter I wrote. I remember it felt like my final good-bye kiss and hug.

> Dear Grandma,
>
> I can't believe you are no longer here to hold my hand and wipe my face, to share apple pie, lollipops, and jelly sandwiches. Thank you for taking off the

ends. I will think of you and me together in the park, and your pushing me on the swings. You always pushed me the best because you knew just how high I wanted to go. You always did everything just the right amount. I'll try and be a big boy and not cry. I know you wouldn't want my tears, but would want me to be brave. When I go to sleep at night, I'll think of our time in front of your window and all the stories you told me about living in England. I'll imagine us flying kites and watching the trains rush through the station. I hope that you're happy where you are. Someday, we'll be happy in heaven together.

I love you,
XXOO Jamie

I remember when reading my letter that day, I felt a cool breeze to my right side, and I immediately looked up to my father and told him, "Grandma is all right. She is close by." It was my grandmother who gave me my first true appreciation that love never dies, and neither do we. To this day, I think about those days by the window, and still miss her.

SIBLINGS

If you have the fortune to share life with a brother or sister, you know that the opportunities and challenges of having siblings give us a different perspective on life. They not only help us to recognize both positive and negative traits about ourselves, but they remind us of our part in the family dynamics. Even though we are part of the same family, our brothers and sisters are unique individuals with their own belief systems and lessons to learn. We can be the best of friends or the worst of enemies. At those times when life throws us a curveball, there is no one better than a brother or sister to empathize with our dilemma and understand what we are going through. They are the only ones who give us sound advice. Because our siblings influence us more than most people, we may come to expect more from them. All too often our expectations exceed reality.

When a brother or sister dies, it may seem like the death of our best friend. Depending on our unique relationship with a sibling, we may feel that the moments of fun and closeness once shared with this person who understood us the most have ended too soon. The thought of existing without our brother or sister is not only unsettling but also fearful. For even if we weren't close on the physical level, on another level we feel as though a part of us has died with them.

From a spiritual point of view, your family members are with you in this life for several reasons. First of all, you belong to a "soul group," and the members of your family are souls with whom you have experienced many lifetimes. All of you have probably participated in different family positions throughout various existences. You have shared many lessons of a spiritual nature. For instance, your sister or brother may be the catalyst for your learning a lesson in understanding. All the members of your family have their own growth and spiritual lessons to experience. The family circle is the optimum choice for such opportunities. This type of arrangement is usually decided in the spiritual realms in between lifetimes. It is there that we evaluate our spiritual growth and determine what we still need to learn. Together with these souls known as our family, we will be able to have the necessary opportunities when we can conquer our fears, overcome our prejudices, and balance our egos.

Second, you may have shared past incarnations with your

family members and must work off karma from another life in this lifetime. Think of karma as a sort of debt that must be repaid. Karma does not always have to be negative. It can be good karma, too. So, we come back into a particular position in the family unit in order to be able to experience or go through our karmic debt with the other family member. I have often described it as going back to earth and taking a class together. The death of a sibling may be painful if the sibling passes without the opportunity you both needed for a spiritual lesson. On an unconscious level, you may feel that you have missed this opportunity, and it leaves you devastated. Here again, you must understand that you will be together again to experience any missed opportunities as well as new possibilities for growth.

Although they are no longer with you in the physical realm, siblings and other family members will take a keen interest in your continued spiritual growth from the spiritual realms. Often they will become guides to you, helping you through this classroom of earth as best they can. And why wouldn't they? Families are especially bound together in spirit. Your love and understanding of each other has crossed over eons of time and a variety of experiences. That's pretty remarkable, if you think about it.

 HEALING GUIDELINES

- Allow yourself to go through the complete grieving process.
- Talk to your siblings about the loss of your parent. Each one will be reacting in his or her own unique way. No one

grieves the same, so don't place your own expectations on other family members. Above all, don't blame each other, or project guilt on to one another for something a person did or didn't do. This is a time to heal wounds among family members, not to create new ones. Come together as one.

- Review your relationship with the deceased. What have you learned from him? How has she made a difference in your life? Are you proud of something that your parent, grandparent, sister, brother, or other relative has given you? Make a list of all the positive attributes of your loved one.

- If there is any unfinished business with a family member, write a letter and describe how you feel. You can even talk out loud. Once you can release your negative feelings, there is room in your heart for love to enter and grow.

- If you were living with your parent at the end, the loss may be particularly difficult. Realize that you are your own person. You are not your parent. You have to take stock of your own life and the ways in which you want to live it. You no longer have to do it your parent's way.

- Forgive your parent for any faults. Your parent was trying to do his best with the information and experience he had. Parents carry on in ways that are familiar to them. If your parent wasn't able to express love and affection, forgive her. Release them so you can begin to express yourself emotionally in ways you never did before.

- If your other parent is still alive, be there for him. If necessary, explain that the death is not her fault. Help your parent to express feelings by talking together. Help to go through your deceased parent's personal belongings. It's okay to share fond memories together because this helps the healing process.

- Understand that you will *not* die at the same age as your parent or have the same problems at the end. You are an individual on your own unique spiritual path.
- Realize it is not the end of the world and that death is a natural process. When all else fails, breathe in and breathe out a few times. This helps to center yourself.
- Thank your parent for giving you life. Thank your brother or sister for sharing life with you. You may want to donate to a charity in his memory, or remember her life by planting a tree, or writing a poem, or through a painting or other form of artistic expression.

4

PARTNERS IN LIFE

*C*oming home to an empty house may be one of the hardest things to handle for a grieving spouse. When your partner dies, it feels as though your whole world has crumbled into pieces. Initially numbness sets in, as if you are living in a foreign country and no one speaks your language. You feel out of control or that you are having a nightmare from which you cannot wake. You wander around as if asleep, and yet overwhelming sadness brings you back to reality. Your loved one is gone, and you feel incomplete and vulnerable. There is no one to motivate you to get up in the morning or to convince you to go to sleep at night. In fact, you cannot face going to bed alone at all. This is part of the normal grieving process.

Losing your mate is in a way losing part of yourself. You have relied on one another, have been intimate with each other, and have supported each other through thick and thin. Now when you need your partner the most, you are alone. Everything you have built together seems meaningless and empty. You wonder what is it all for if there is no one to share it with. It doesn't matter if you were together several months or seventy years, a cherished part of life has been taken away. It almost seems impossible to be a part of a world without the one you love.

This became quite evident to me when my mother passed away. She and my father enjoyed a loving relationship for forty years. Looking back over their relationship, I remember my siblings and me joking about them being like Archie and Edith in the television show *All in the Family*. Teasing and kidding were their way of communicating with one another. My father never overtly displayed an enormous amount of affection toward my mother, but the love was present as part of their mutual bantering back and forth. Just like the Bunkers, they had fallen into a comfortable routine with each other. Were they the ideal couple? No, I'm sure they were not. They probably thought of going their separate ways many times in their relationship. But that was never really an option. People back then didn't divorce as easily as they do now. When you married, you married for better or worse for the rest of your life.

On the day my mother died, my father was not the man I had known all my life. He looked like someone who had been swallowed up whole. He was totally out of control, visibly rattled, and so unlike his easygoing and steady self. No one in my family had ever seen my dad as distressed as he was that day.

I don't think my father has ever really gotten over my mom's death. He still misses her terribly. He talks for hours about what they used to do when they first started dating. He reminisces about the good old days—the songs he and Mom used to dance to, the places they used to visit, and the friends they used to go out with. He calls her name all the time and spends a good part of the day staring at her picture. I think he is waiting for her to talk back somehow to him. If my father never openly expressed his love for my mother while she was alive, he has certainly made up for it since she died. I am still amazed at the amount of undying love he has for her. I think he will only be truly happy when he is with her again in spirit. I think then the part of him that died in 1985 will be reborn, and that old charming smile of his will return once again.

 ## FINDING EMOTIONAL SUPPORT

In many cultures and traditions around the world, there are healthy outlets to deal with the loss of a partner. Societies recognize the need for emotionally supporting the surviving spouse with rituals and customs that last weeks, even months after the death. In our country, however, losing a spouse almost becomes a cut-and-dried business. A widow or widower has to immediately begin to fill out form after form, as if she or he were moving shares of stock. There is no real time-out for the spouse to grieve. A person has to tidy up affairs with the bank, the hospital, the doctors, the mortuary, and the Social Security office. Everything must be back to business as usual within a few short days of the death. This is hardly the way to help a grieving person cope with his or her sorrow.

Because of all the turmoil one faces at such a time, a surviving partner needs to find someone who can be his or her emotional pillar of strength. This could be a best friend, a family member, or even someone in a grief-support group. I believe this is the very first step a surviving individual should take; it is of vital importance to have a support system to help bear the weight of the grief. The support person is there to help you, so you *do not* have to go through it alone—someone with whom you can talk about the death, and discuss the funeral arrangements, and help with the paperwork.

Another essential part of having a support person is to keep the grieving individual in balance. The aftereffect of death can alter someone's lifestyle and daily routine dramatically. Daily tasks and simple everyday chores such as using a washing machine or dishwasher, buying groceries and preparing meals, driving a car, and paying bills are often overwhelming for a surviving spouse, especially one who was completely dependent on the other. The once common acts of eating a meal or going to sleep create untold sadness and agony for many. Fear, loneliness, feeling sick, insomnia, worry, and exhaustion have taken the place of a familiar mate. Some grieving spouses are thrown into an emotional tailspin, and any number of reactions can rise to the surface. It is important that one be aware of certain danger signals, such as thoughts of suicide. Other feelings of isolation and despair may also need therapeutic attention.

I often meet widows and widowers who find it difficult to ask someone for help. They see it as a form of weakness, and some just won't do it. This is especially true as people get on in years and have become set in their ways. For them, asking for help is like admitting dependency or giving up control. But seeking assistance from someone can be amazingly helpful. Facing the loss of a spouse or partner is enough of an emotional strain to bear. Adding everyday stresses on top of it only prolongs the suffering. I know it can be difficult to let someone new into your life after the one you love is gone. After all, how can you explain to anyone the bond you shared with your partner? But please don't be afraid to ask for help. There are people just waiting to assist you.

SOUL DEVELOPMENT

The experiences of life are vast and varied, and we try our best to understand and explore the twists and turns on our journey through it. For every rough time there is always a sweet and effortless experience waiting for us on the other side. This is the nature of life. Despite it all, we always hope for a better tomorrow. I have found that in the midst of such chaos, there is an order to life. When we interfere with that order by hanging on to our fears and feelings of limitation, it seems as if our lives do not work out as well as we would like. When one has to deal with a challenge like the death of spouse, one can hardly see any good coming from it. Instead, we feel shut off from any sort of happiness coming our way. However, a special opportunity for tremendous growth stands at our doorstep. What we perceive as destructive and depressing can become a major turning point. No matter what we may think, it is certainly never meant to be the end.

A common theme throughout my readings is that we come back to this earth to learn lessons for our personal soul development, and one of the most common lessons is that of love. There are many forms of love. Sharing a life with someone is one way to understand and develop an aspect of love. A relationship brings necessary lessons for each individual that are usually based on karmic ties of former lifetimes. These lessons help us to advance both individually and as part of a group on a soul path.

Sometimes we are not able to complete our lessons in this life for a variety of reasons. In the first reading, a spouse was unable to cope with life and trust in her capabilities. She was chemically dependent and chemically imbalanced. Her course of action changed the direction of the other spouse's life and that of her children. In the next reading, the couple was able to fulfill their karmic lessons together. They were able to blend their thoughts, ideas and beliefs and merge into one unit through understanding and love. For them life was indeed beautiful. When each person is able to fulfill his or her mission in life through the aid of the other, that becomes love in its highest form. The third reading in this chapter touches on yet another of life's lessons—completing past-life karma. The bonds of love that we make in one life keep reuniting us until we have mastered what we have agreed to learn.

No matter what the karmic lesson of the relationship, those who survive the death have the difficult task of facing the emotional, physical, and spiritual sides of life without their loved one by their side.

MY PROTECTOR

On a recent tour for my second book, *Reaching to Heaven*, I appeared on a television show in which the producers wanted me to read for several people on stage as well as in the audience. I remember that it was a rough day for me, as it was the last stop on a twenty-city tour. The producers knew it was good television for me to do readings, but like most people, they are completely unaware of how much energy it takes to do this kind of work and how fickle spirits can be. Even if a person has a deep desire to contact a loved one, I cannot guarantee that a spirit will present itself to a particular person. However, I also know that through my demonstrations people have a better understanding of life after death, and hopefully have less fear about dying.

As with all the TV shows I do, I had no advance knowledge about an individual's personal life before the reading. Halfway through this particular presentation, I was drawn to a man sitting on the side. He did not seem to be someone very open to this type of experience. As I walked toward him, he smiled sweetly at me.

"Hello, I'm James," I said to him.

"Ralph," was his reply.

I explained that a spirit wanted to communicate to him. I said a prayer, tuned into his energy, and immediately felt an incredible amount of grief and anguish. Then I looked into this man's dark eyes and saw a lot of sadness.

I began to slowly quiet my mind and enter a receptive state, or, as I like to say, *I open the door to spirit.* Quickly two bright gold rings appeared over Ralph's head.

"I am seeing two gold rings joined together over your head. When I see this, it usually means a marriage. I assume you have a wife in spirit?"

Before he had time to answer, I saw a tall dark-haired woman coming into focus. When I see a vision like this, it appears to me much like focusing the lens of a camera. The woman stood on his right side and reached out for his shoulder. It looked as though she had been crying.

"Your wife is here," I said.

He nodded his head firmly in agreement.

"She is giving me the impression of children. She misses her children. Are there two girls?"

"Yes," he replied, his eyes beginning to tear.

I continued sensing the spirit of his wife, and then I let out a sigh.

"Your wife is very sad. I feel very sad. Her emotional state is not good. I feel she is still despondent. She is so sorry for causing you and your girls so much pain. I feel like she is new in spirit, like she has been there less than a year."

Ralph acknowledged this with a nod of his head.

"She is showing me a Christmas tree and telling me she had something to do with Christmas. Do you understand this?" I asked.

"Yes, she died the day after Christmas."

I suddenly felt metal in my mouth. To me, this always means that a gun is involved. I knew that she was the one who used a gun and that somebody else did not shoot her. I knew this was a suicide for two reasons. First, I could feel the disturbed emotional state of the individual. Second, I could sense that she had possession of the weapon. In other instances I am visually shown the details of the event.

I conveyed this to Ralph. "She gives me the feeling that she shot herself with a gun."

"That's right," Ralph mumbled as he rubbed his eyes. A gasp rose in the audience.

"Your wife is telling me that she couldn't finish her work down here. She said that she could not mentally handle the life she laid out for herself. She was unable to keep things in balance."

Ralph nodded his head up and down again. "I knew that. I knew she couldn't handle it. I picked up on that right after we got married."

"Your wife gives me the feeling that she was on drugs, like medication, to handle mood swings. Did she get depressed a lot?" I asked.

"Yes, she did. She was on Zoloft for her depression. She was also seeing a therapist," Ralph answered.

"I think she had a chemical imbalance. This is the feeling she is conveying to me."

Ralph seemed to agree.

"She is telling me that you both agreed to be together in this lifetime to learn about intimacy and trust. She is so sorry she couldn't fulfill her promise. She says you will share another lifetime together. There will be another chance, she is saying. She wants me to tell you that she is working on herself to get better."

Ralph was very happy to hear that, and asked, "Does she know how much I think about her, and that I will always love her?"

After a few moments I gave his wife's response.

"Yes. She can read your thoughts, and is telling me that your love has been built over the ages. She knows that you hold a place in your heart for her. She says to tell you that you have always been her protector, not only this life but in past times as well. She will always call you her protector."

Everyone in the room was sensitive to the communication of love between these two people. There was complete silence.

I then explained in detail how spirits are always aware of our thoughts and feelings. In fact, they are even more aware of them than we realize because spirits live in a mental world and receive impressions of thought from the plane we live on and the spirit plane simultaneously.

"Your wife is talking about one daughter coloring a picture of her. Do you understand this?"

"Yeah. Jody did a crayon drawing of my wife for school. She actually won an award for it. It's hanging on the refrigerator."

I looked Ralph straight in the eye and said, "Your wife

wants you to get a puppy for the kids. She has been trying to impress your mind with this thought."

"Yeah, I know. Just yesterday I was talking about it with the kids, but I don't know—"

I interrupted him before he could finish. "She is telling me that it's important because it will help the children with their grief. They can express their love for another creature and learn about love from it."

Ralph smiled, but he didn't seem so keen on the idea. The energy in the room started to fade. I could tell it was getting more difficult to feel and hear the wife's thoughts. There was one last message that she wanted to convey.

"Your wife wants to talk to you about the couch. She is with you when you are watching television at night. Do you understand this? She says you no longer have to fight over flipping the channels. She is still with you on the couch."

Ralph's face brightened. "I feel her with me. We used to watch TV together every night, and we would argue about what to watch. Eventually we would agree on a show, and she would always fall asleep with my arms wrapped around her, protecting her."

With that, we gave each other a smile of understanding and shook hands.

Later, I found out the whole story from Ralph about him and his wife, Stacey. Ralph told me that he grew up in Brooklyn. He met his wife at college, and they dated for several years before they married. After five years they had two little girls, Jody and Debbie. Ralph worked in the office of the district attorney. He was dedicated to his job, got several promotions, and was able to buy a beautiful home in a New York suburb. He thought life was as perfect as it could get. He said that he and Stacey were living the typical American dream, filled with

Girl Scout outings and PTA meetings. It seemed like the good life, or so Ralph thought.

He said that one afternoon he came home from work and found Stacey sleeping in bed. The house was a mess, and the children were hungry. Ralph knew something was wrong.

"She was going through a lot of mood swings lately, but this was the first time I saw her like this."

Stacey explained to Ralph that it was sort of a mid-life crisis. At first Ralph didn't think much about it, but then Stacey's mood swings became more frequent.

One day Ralph left work at lunchtime. "It was one of those rare occasions when I got out of work early, and I wanted to surprise Stacey."

Ralph told me that he entered the house through the back door. "I noticed it was too quiet," he said. "I thought I heard a moan coming from down in the basement. I opened the basement door and started to walk down the steps."

Ralph said that as he reached the bottom step, he saw a dark shadow in the corner of the room. "With the sunlight filtering through a small window, I could make out the figure of Stacey leaning against the wall."

As Ralph walked closer, he was shocked to see Stacey in a fetal position. "I couldn't believe my eyes. There was a belt around her biceps and a syringe on the floor. I knelt down and called her name."

But Stacey was too far gone for Ralph to get through to her. "She looked like she was in another world far away, so I screamed at her, but she still couldn't wake up from her stupor."

He said that he knew he had to get help immediately, so he carried her upstairs and called the paramedics. Stacey was rushed to the hospital and, luckily, saved from a drug overdose.

That's when Ralph found out that Stacey had been a heroin addict for over a year.

He said, "The pills she was taking for her mood swings didn't seem to help her cope anymore. She said she felt worse as each day went by. I think she was afraid of getting old." Ralph mentioned that some boyfriend of Stacey's best friend turned his wife on to heroin.

After Stacey's near-fatal overdose, she promised Ralph that she would go into rehab. "For a while things seemed to return to normal."

But Ralph still sensed that something was wrong. "I couldn't put my finger on it," he said. Yet the feeling ate away at him. Then everything came to an end one early morning, the day after Christmas.

Ralph was awakened in the middle of the night. "I heard a single popping sound."

At three-thirty in the morning, Ralph found his wife slumped on the bathroom floor. "She had just blown her head off."

UPDATE

My reading with Ralph occurred about a year ago. Since then I have talked with him about his ongoing grieving process.

"I still miss Stacey a lot, but to know that she is alive and still with us in some way has really helped me," he said.

He also mentioned that he has been able to talk about his feelings with friends who knew all about Stacey and her drug addiction. "Talking about it with people who knew what I had been through has helped me tremendously," he told me.

Ralph continued, saying that he encourages his children to talk to their mother, but none of them seem to need any urging. "The girls understand that their mom is an angel and is always around watching out for them.

"I still celebrate her birthday," he said.

Ralph said that he now understands that there was a reason for this experience.

He then said something that surprised me. "I'm ready to think about finding someone to love someday. It will be hard to fill Stacey's shoes, but I'm willing to give it a try." Ralph and I both agreed that this was a sign of progress.

He said, "Stacey still communicates with me. Sometimes I feel her around; other times, something falls off the shelf, and I know it's her."

Ralph said that he and the girls have dreams of Stacey, and she appears to be happy and more at peace. In one dream Stacey walked with Ralph around a wood cabin that was decorated with handmade furniture and beautiful hanging art. As he looked out the window of this cabin, he saw a lake that was familiar to him.

He told me, "That dream meant a lot to me." He and Stacey had always talked about saving money to buy a cabin by the lake. He felt that Stacey had built the house in spirit. "One day we will be together again to enjoy it."

SURVIVORS OF SUICIDE

In my first book, *Talking to Heaven,* I devoted a chapter to the spiritual view of suicide. Since then I have had many people question me about their loved ones who have committed suicide. The most common theme of these questions has to do with a person lingering in some purgatory or hell because of committing suicide. Often survivors of suicide victims feel very guilty, as if there were something they could have done to prevent the act. This is understandable although misguided.

Suicide is a complicated issue, and there are many reasons why it occurs. Spirits usually communicate in readings that they have regret for their actions. Many souls who commit suicide in this lifetime have committed suicide in a past life. They return to overcome the inclination to commit suicide, but are unable to accomplish what they set out to do. They will return again and be given another opportunity to master this lesson.

Then there are souls who commit suicide who have mental and biochemical imbalances. Stacey was one of them. These souls are not fully conscious of their decisions. When they pass over, they find themselves in a sort of hospital where they can be helped.

A few souls return too quickly to the physical realm. I touch on this idea in *Reaching to Heaven*. These souls have not had enough preparation in the spiritual realms to return to earth fully aware of their lessons, and when they get here, they realize they have returned prematurely. These souls know that they just don't fit in and are not really ready to spend another lifetime in the physical realm.

When a person commits suicide, there is much he has to learn on the other side before moving into the higher heaven realms. Once one becomes aware of the suicide, she has the free will to ask for help. Spirit guides are always around to assist those in need. It is always up to each individual soul to learn from one's mistakes and progress in the spirit world. That is why I always tell people to continue to pray for those who have passed over. Your prayers do not only comfort them, but the love and intention behind the prayers helps them to move forward on their spiritual paths.

LOVE KNOWS NO LIMIT

Humans know that love exists, but so many don't know what love is. Think of all the times you have said to yourself or to someone else: *I love you. I love my children. I love my work.* I'm sure that we all can give examples of acts of love and testify to the depth of love we have for someone or something, but can we describe it accurately? We feel it, we think it, we romanticize it, and we experience it, yet when asked to define it, we come up short. Why is love so difficult to define? Probably because the answer is too simple for us to understand.

Love is everything. It is the energy of the Universe. It is the divine, unseen, unifying force that holds everything together. It is in us, around us, and connects us. Love belongs to everyone and everything; there are no boundaries, belief systems, religious or political ideology, or prejudice that can control or manipulate love. It is the only *real* thing that exists, and each of us is made of it. Yet we often find love difficult to recognize within ourselves or anyone else.

We are all a part of this one consciousness of love. When we are able to understand that everyone is composed of this same divine element, we will be able to open the door to this God Force energy in every aspect of our lives. The more we release our judgments, and the more we begin to respect the other guy for who he is, a child of God, the more our spiritual vibration will become bright and pure. The more we align to love, the closer we come to God or our God consciousness. Each one has the opportunity on this earth to use the divine energy of love. As inconceivable as it may seem, by honoring and respecting each other we are really loving ourselves. But few are willing to move into this loving consciousness wholeheartedly. Instead we are only willing to give and receive love piecemeal, and many are capable of giving only with the hope of getting something in return. This is love based on conditions. The love of which I speak is unconditional. It is all-giving and all encompassing. It is not some sort of an investment where a return is expected.

When you turn the word love around, you get "evol." One must *love* in order to *evolve* spiritually. As light beings, we are recognized not by the amount of intelligence we possess, or our acquired wealth, or public or political status, but only by our capacity to love. The intelligence of the heart goes far beyond this mortal realm.

I have found in doing my readings that when a spirit comes through on a loving vibration, the message is one of clarity and pureness. The information comes through effortlessly. There is a joyful feeling surrounding the communication. I always tell a client that it is the love bond between her and her deceased loved one that helps a spirit communicate. It is quite amazing to hear a spirit describe how much love there is in the spirit world. Often a spirit mentions how much further he would have progressed on a spiritual level if he had used more love while on earth. Many spirits speak about the need to love others and to love themselves as well. They consistently communicate again and again: *It is never too late to begin to love.*

I want to share with you a session that occurred some years ago. It concerns an elderly couple, Margaret, known to her friends as "Margie," and Bart, known to his friends as "Buddy." Margie and Buddy met each other in high school and stayed together the rest of their lives. They had been married fifty-two years. In my estimation, Margie and Buddy's life illustrates the great capacity two human beings have for love. Buddy and Margie loved each other unconditionally, and through their example have taught others that with love all things are possible. Their story demonstrates how to live positively and abundantly, foregoing other people's expectations, fears, and illusions that often stand in the way of love. Instead of living by society's standards, Margie and Buddy lived by the rules of the heart. Their love validates that there is love even in death, and that with love, we are never alone.

Like most married couples, this unique twosome had experienced all the ups and downs that life usually offers. They had lived through world wars, bankruptcy, sickness, deaths, children, and grandchildren. They had their share of jobs, houses, and vacations, good times, bad times, and everything else in between. After reading for Margie, I sat a couple of hours with her, not wanting to leave her company. There was a strange and unique sweetness about her. She was and still is quite a lady and a great teacher of life.

I remember her saying, "James, you must slow down and not take on the whole world. You mustn't care about those who don't believe in your work and what they say. Their own limitations stop them from seeing the truth." Those words have rung true time and again for me. I have learned a lot from Margie, as had so many others. After the reading I felt as though she had given me a lot more than I had given her. I felt enlightened by her presence.

When I first sat down with Margie, I didn't think she needed a reading. She seemed so together; I didn't think anything from the spirit world would change her perspective on life. I knew she didn't come to me in sheer desperation. Rather, she just wanted to talk once again to the person in her life who taught her how to love. She wanted to speak with her soul mate Buddy, who had died two years before from lung cancer. At the same time, Buddy was on the other side waiting to talk to her. I remember Margie straightening her dress in a dignified manner as I began the reading.

"There is a gentleman standing on your left side, and he wants to hold your hand."

"That's Buddy, all right. He always wanted to hold my hand. He is so fresh," she confessed with a giggle.

"He is wearing a brown suit," I continued. "He says he didn't want you to upstage him by dressing up. He is very sweet. He is laughing as well. He is showing me a medal on his lapel."

"Oh, geez, does he still have that darn thing?" Margie turned to the left and shrieked, "Buddy, I put that thing in the pine coffin. Couldn't you have left it there?"

I had to wait for his reply. I saw Buddy holding a bouquet of flowers for Margie.

"He is giving you purple irises."

The stalwart expression on Margie's face disappeared, and teardrops fell on her cheeks.

"They are my favorite flowers. He bought them for me every anniversary and every birthday. As a matter of fact, we planted some a couple of weeks before he died. I miss him, you know."

"Yes, I understand." I felt her sadness.

Margie interrupted, "That metal was a Purple Heart. He got it during World War II. He saved a whole battalion of men."

She turned her head toward the floor, in what I thought was a deep moment of contemplation. Suddenly she looked back up and yelled out, "He was such a fool. But that was the way he was. Anyone needing a hand, even if it was something he knew nothing about, he would try and help."

"Buddy wants you to know that there are wonderful people in the spirit world. He has met many old friends of yours. He has seen Mae and your mom and dad. He says they are still the same. Your father is keen on seeing now."

Margie cried, "Oh, good old Mae. She's my sister. She's been dead for ten years. My father was blind for most of his adult life. There was an accident in his factory. The poor man suffered so much. It makes me very happy to know that he can see again. That was so long ago, yet it seems like yesterday."

"Buddy is telling me that he visits you all the time. He is telling me that he was with you when you heard 'Blue Moon,' and wanted to dance with you."

"That was our favorite song. Every time we heard it, he would quickly pull me up on my feet and start to dance, just like when we first met."

Margie looked off to the side, remembering the good old days. "I heard that song on the radio the other night. You know," she said as she looked at me, "I knew he was standing next to me, waiting to dance. I felt it. I could smell his cologne and practically felt his hand touch mine. I thought it was an old lady's imagination."

I told her, "He was there. He is telling me that it was real."

I continued, "Buddy wants me to tell you that he feels like a kid again. And by the way, he says he saw you throw out some pills recently. He is laughing and saying, 'That's my gal.'"

Margie laughed back and said, "Oh, yes, for high blood pressure. I just figured I have lived this long without them. I don't think it would really make a difference. I think doctors still have a lot to learn. They tend to give people too much medication. God has given us a remedy for everything. I've been taking herbs for years, and I am eighty-seven years old."

We went on for some time without looking at the clock. Margie was certainly a character and quite an old soul. Buddy came through with details about their children and grandchildren. He spoke of their trips together, the greyhounds they used to raise, and all the fun they shared in life. They spoke of loving each other regardless of their personal mannerisms and faults.

Margie responded, "Too many people live in fear and judgment. They have to overlook a lot of the minor stuff that happens in a relationship and focus on the love. It's the only way to survive and grow."

Margie and Buddy talked about their relationship being simple and not being messed up with complications.

The reading was enlightening and emotional. There was so much I got out of it. Toward the end of the session, something touched me deeply.

"Your husband wants you to say hello to Hank."

"Oh, Hank. Yes, I will. He's not you, Buddy, a little slow, but he is a kind man. And by the way, he fixes everything in the house. It was a good idea, Buddy."

I received a flash of the Las Vegas strip, so I asked Margie if this meant anything.

"Oh, yes. Hank and I got married there."

I was confused because I knew that Buddy was her husband.

"Oh yes, Buddy is my husband, and Hank is, too. An old lady with two husbands!" She flashed a confident smile.

"Buddy and I were married for over fifty years. We knew one day one of us would have to pass on. We loved each other very much. Buddy was rarely ill, but when he got cancer, we knew it was the end. Buddy didn't want me to be alone in my old age. He said that if he couldn't remain here to take care of me, he wanted someone else to be with me and keep me company. So we looked around our retirement community."

Margie let out a small laugh, enjoying an inside joke. "We found three gentlemen who we thought would be suitable. They were all widowers. Buddy and I discussed their good points and their bad. We thought Fred was too needy, and Joe too religious a man. I am not a religious person. I believe God is in your heart, not in a church. Anyway, Hank was the fix-it man around the complex, and we liked each other, he more than me, of course. So Buddy asked Hank if he would take care of me when he was gone. Hank agreed, and several months after Buddy's passing, we got married in Vegas. The ladies at the complex think Hank is a dirty old man. Ha, if they only knew the truth."

I was amazed at the thought that Buddy would prearrange Margie's affair so that she would have a companion after he passed over. It was a great lesson about sharing and letting go at the same time. Neither Margie nor Buddy cared what the neighbors thought; nor did they let their pride or ego stand in the way of their love for each other.

The last thing Buddy said to Margie was, "Next time you hear 'Blue Moon,' picture me standing in front of you, reaching for your hand and asking you for a dance."

Buddy truly captured the moment. My feeling is that their dancing days, like their love, will go on forever.

UPDATE

The last time I spoke with Margie, she and her husband Hank had moved to Las Vegas. Margie always said she was a lucky gambler, and felt Buddy was giving her a hand at the slot machines. She and Hank are spending their golden years traveling around the country. "He's my best friend now," Margie said of Hank. "We like doing the same sort of things and enjoy each other's companionship. We're what you might call good roommates." As we ended our conversation, Margie reminded me of one last thing: "I think Hank, Buddy, and I will all be together in the hereafter, and that suits me fine."

GUIDANCE FROM ABOVE

Part of the meaningfulness of my being involved in after-death communication and grief counseling is to experience the profound and the sacred. When I open myself to the spiritual dimensions, I never know who will communicate or what will manifest from the interaction. Most of my readings contain evidential details that validate a genuine communication with a client and a loved one that confirms the survival of consciousness beyond the passage of death. There are those rare times, though, when other beings reveal themselves during a reading. Often they bestow soulful insights to help a client expand his or her own spiritual awareness. Many years ago, I experienced one of these exceptional moments. It was a session that not only changed my client's perspective of life but mine as well. As I sit here and write this book, I realize that the particular session that follows was meant not only for the woman who came one spring afternoon in 1993, but was to be shared with the rest of the world.

In presenting the following, my hope is that you will reflect upon the information with an open mind. If it resonates within your being, apply it to your own life, and see how it changes your preconceived ideas and knowledge. Perhaps it is the key that you need right now to discover your own happiness and understanding. I believe the reading demonstrates that the power of love and only love can help to free us from the trappings of past experiences and to live in oneness and the true and pure sense of joyful wholeness. As with all the sessions I recount in my books, I will attempt to convey not only the detailed information and insightfulness of the session, but will reiterate some of the heartfelt emotions that transpired between both dimensions.

The doorbell rang at five minutes before two. I had just fin-ished wolfing down a tuna fish sandwich. I was in the process of centering myself before the client arrived, but she was five minutes early. The noise of the bell shook me back to aware-ness, and I quickly ran to the door. An attractive blonde-haired woman introduced herself as Susan. When she smiled, I noticed her perfect white teeth, which matched her perfect model face and figure. I invited her into my living room and asked her to make herself comfortable.

After I was sure that she understood the way spirit commu-nication took place, I began to sense a "denseness" of energy in the room. This is a very common occurrence. I have noticed that the energy in the room begins to change as I am about to do a reading, and often before the client arrives. I believe this is the energy of "spirit workers" who come to assist in the man-ifestation of spirit communication.

Usually I ask that a client not share information with me prior to a reading. I prefer that my thoughts not be colored with a client's desires and expectations. In Susan's case, she had an overwhelming urge to talk to me. Clients are usually nervous when they arrive because they have never done this sort of thing. As she sat down, Susan said, "I hope you can help me, James. I have had some horrific nightmares. I pray before I go to sleep, but it doesn't seem to help. I also feel like I am never alone in my room, like someone is watching me. It's kind of freaky."

I assured her that everything would be all right and began to go into a meditative state. I tuned in to the energy around her and immediately felt the presence of a lady with a German accent.

"Trudy sends you love and is watching over you. Don't worry, nothing is going to harm you."

I found out that Trudy was Susan's grandmother, and she was a spiritualist in Germany at the turn of the century.

"She is saying that she now works in the spirit world with people who pass with experiences of being physically handicapped while on earth. She does her best to help them adjust to their new life of freedom in the spiritual dimensions."

This made sense to Susan because Grandma Trudy worked in a hospital as a physical therapist.

At one point Trudy said to me, "The room is crowded. There are others here who need to speak with Susan. They have been waiting a long time for this moment."

We thanked Trudy, and I waited for more impressions from the spirit world.

After a few moments a man came through who seemed a little "off." He was cradling his head with his left hand.

"There is a man standing behind you. His face is pure white, and he is holding his head on the left side, right next to his ear. He looks like a zombie because he is just staring at me. I am sending him a thought, but he doesn't want to respond, or can't."

Susan suddenly became shaken by this remark.

I continued. "This is strange. I am seeing a beach. It looks like a beach at night, and there's a full moon. I can see it reflected on the water. This man is in silhouette. He is looking from a window out toward the water."

I looked at Susan and said, "It reminds me of Malibu Beach."

"Yes, please go on," she said anxiously.

"He is now walking toward a bookshelf. He is turning around, and his mouth is open like he wants to say something. He is swatting at something with his hand. I don't know what it means. Now he seems to be screaming. He is falling down and holding his head. All I can see now is a pool of blood on the carpet. His head is sitting in a pool of blood."

Susan let out a scream. "That's my nightmare! Make it *stop*. Please, make it stop."

I was shaken, too. The details were so vivid in my mind. I felt I was looking at a photograph. I knew that I had just witnessed what had to be a murder, and I felt very odd. Most of the time I am all right when witnessing deaths because I am an observer, not a participant. In this scenario I felt immediately involved and upset.

After a few moments Susan blew her nose and said, "Why did it have to happen?"

I did my best to reassure her that the event was over, and nothing could harm her. I began to see a ring, not a regular ring, but three rings intertwined into one. I asked Susan if this meant something.

"Yes. That's right. We bought them in Big Bear right after we met and used them as our wedding bands."

"I don't know what this means, but I hear something like 'Bobo.' I think that is what I am getting. Do you understand that name?" I asked.

"Yes, that's my husband. His real name is Bobby, but I called him Bobo. No one ever called him that except me. I miss him. I miss him so much."

The previous vision had faded, and I was filled with a strong sense of compassion from this man, mixed with layers of emotion.

"This man Bobo seems quite an unhappy sort of guy. I am sorry, but he seems very lost, like he has been forgotten. He seems to be crying and crying. I feel as though I can't continue until he stops. There is so much sadness with him. He feels as though he let you down."

Susan looked over to my side and spoke to Bobo directly. "I'm here, sweetie. You know I am always here for you. And I always will be."

"I get a sense of him in a fetal position lying on a bed. The cover of the bed is yellowish with small red and pink flowers. I see red pillows, too."

She exclaimed, "That's my bed! I have that bedspread and the red pillows. Oh, my God. Is that where he is? Bobo, is that you in bed?"

"Was he a very controlling man?" I asked. "Because he seems as if he was a bit rough and always wanted things his way. He didn't take no for an answer."

"Yes, James. I guess you could say that. But I always knew how to handle him. It's funny; I was the only one he wouldn't yell at. But at work, forget it. He was a tyrant and fired people all the time."

"He is mentioning something about show business. Was he in the movie business?"

"Well, he was a music agent. We used to hang out with a lot of people in show business."

Then some very intriguing information was revealed.

"He is giving me the name of Kristine or Kristel with a K. Do you know this person?" I asked.

Susan stared down at the wall beside her left foot. Tears started to well up in her eyes. She looked at me and mouthed, "Yeah. I understand. What about it?"

"He keeps saying he is sorry. You were right. He is sorry. He let you down. He wants you to know he loves you."

"So, it's true?" she inquired.

"Yes, he is saying it is true, and that he is very sorry. You knew it."

Susan started to cry. "I felt it, but I didn't want to believe it.

How could he do that to me? Didn't he know how much I loved him? I could have had anyone, but I stuck it out with him."

"Do you know this woman?" I asked.

"Yes, I met her a while back. She wasn't at his funeral. Some people at work said that after Bobby died, she moved back East with her family."

The reading continued as Bobo confessed his affair with a coworker named Kristine. He explained that he had met her at a party, and the two of them felt a mutual attraction.

Susan had heard about it after her husband's murder. "I didn't want to believe it."

"He is giving me the name of Dan or Danny. Do you know that name?"

Susan could not place the name. I repeated the name to her, insisting that she must know of this person. "Your husband is quite emphatic about it."

"No, I am sorry, it doesn't mean anything to me."

"Keep it. It may make sense in the future."

This is an extremely common situation in the readings. Usually a sitter has her own expectations of what she will hear and is not open to new or different information.

"He is telling me that Danny knows everything, that he is sitting on a beach in Mexico. He will come from Mexico. Does any of that make sense?"

Susan did not understand what her husband was saying. Several months later, though, the information her dead husband had revealed to her would make complete sense.

I had been sitting in extreme concentration for over fifty minutes and was beginning to tire. I recall looking over to Susan and seeing a woman with a shattered soul. I distinctly remember saying to myself that I had to stop. I was getting very tired, and I didn't want to fall asleep in front of a client. I began to feel very hot and was aware of the sensation of swirling energy all around me. I felt the energy in the room become lighter, and even the appearance of the room took on brighter colors. Blue, violet, and gold lights swirled around the room. Suddenly a man with deep blue eyes climbed into my soul, and I blacked out.

The next thing I saw when I opened my eyes was Susan standing in front of me with a huge smile and a glass of water.

"Are you all right?" she asked.

This could not be the same woman who moments before had been sitting in front of me in a puddle of tears.

"Thank you, James. Thank you so much. You are so wonderful, I can't believe it. You have helped me to understand. It all makes so much sense now."

I didn't know what she meant, and felt as though I was on an episode of *Star Trek*.

"I don't understand."

She told me what had occurred. I had gone into a total unconscious state, and a spirit guide of hers came through to talk to her. This is very rare in my readings.

"Do you mind if I rewind the tape and listen to what your guide said?"

"Of course not," she answered.

I pressed the play button and suddenly heard a deep, melodic voice filled with compassion. There was nothing jarring or disagreeable about his manner, quite the opposite. I have heard myself in a trance state when several of my own guides have come through, but I had never heard this voice before.

"Salutations, dear one. I am with you this day to impart insights for a yearning soul. Your kindness and compassion have lit the heart of your young man, as it has for eons in what you refer to as time. You have walked many roads together in greatness and humility, peace and war, stretching the span of human experience. You have shared expressions as wife and husband, mother and daughter, father, son, sister and brother. You have strung through eternity a strand of diamonds made with your love. You are here today after sharing time and space as partners yet again. Partnership not only in the physical sense, but in the spiritual sense as well. Partners are not limited to husband and wife. Parent and child, friends and lovers are all in partnership working toward fulfillment and growth.

"In this most recent time this soul you know as Bobby returned to the earth with a covenant to you created many lifetimes ago. You have been and continue to be his teacher. This is a role that both of you have found quite suitable, and one in which you are most comfortable. This time your partner found himself reliving old soul patterns that he has played out in many lifetimes. Once again his low self-esteem forced his ego to look elsewhere for love and security instead of going within to his own source of light. He did not understand that his heart had found a place to rest with you, the one he had married. Instead he had an affair with a woman whom he had known from a previous life. He loved this woman then, but it was an unrequited love. In this life, he was compelled to conquer her, and would not take no for an answer. He says now he realizes that he had the perfect love with you; however, it was his ego that kept him from the truth of his being. He was killed by yet another who used control and manipulation to get what he wanted in the world. Your husband was with this woman in her house when he was killed. This was his test, and, as in previous times, it proved to be a fatal one.

"You come with a heavy heart, and it imposes itself not only on you, but on everyone with whom you are in contact physically, spiritually, mentally, and emotionally. I am speaking not only of those existing on your earth, but those of us in the spirit worlds as well. Anyone who has known you and cares for you and loves you feels your upset and your agony, especially the man who you believe has caused all your pain. You, dear one, find it hard to believe that this person who you have loved and to whom you have kept your promise could forsake you for another. You feel cheated. Likewise, you feel it unreasonable that his life be cut short, and you are left to live alone without him. What you see is a reflection of what you have first seen within your own mind. We always project out into the world the thoughts, feelings, and attitudes that preoccupy us. It is up to you to see the world differently by changing your mind about what you want to see. The temptation to react with anger, depression, or excitement exists because of interpretations we make of the external stimuli in our environment. Such interpretations are based on incomplete information.

"Often we look for love in partners, children, parents, and friends. We feel it is easier to love others than self. In a way this satisfies us, but this is a falsehood. In your world you have an illusory power known as fear. Fear is felt when one is not true to oneself. Our fear of not being loved in return blocks us from growing in a total, loving way. This fear is imposed on others, especially the ones we love. Other people do not have to change for us to have peace of mind. It is within our own being that we must first experience this peace. If our state of mind is one of well-being, love, and peace, this is what we will project outward and therefore will experience. If our state of mind is one that is filled with doubts and fear, we will project this state outward, and it will therefore become our reality. When one comes from fear, one is seeing the world from a distorted viewpoint. Do not look to others to satisfy that which is lacking in self.

"Your partner had to learn about loving himself, but he had no idea what this meant. He reverted to his past habits of control and manipulation of others to render them helpless. You wanted to help him to learn and recognize intimacy within himself. He has had trouble with this aspect of himself in the past and was attempting to overcome these tendencies this time around. In order to challenge these aspects of himself, he had to be self-responsible, but instead he indulged in his habits without thinking of the effect they had on others. There is a great difference in a mind that says, 'This is what I want to do' and 'This is what I need to do.' Often what we need to do in order to be a whole, enlightened, and radiant being is not necessarily what we want to do.

"Upon arriving here, your soul partner has had time to reevaluate his life and his earthly tasks. Some progress has been made. Yet he remains fixated on how he did not accomplish as much as he had originally intended. He has imprisoned himself within the trappings of his earthly mind. He is unable to forgive himself for destroying your life as well as his. This soul, like many who come here, realized too late the importance of each day, each moment, each experience on the earth as an opportunity for understanding. He now wishes he had taken the time to live with his heart instead of his head, to see his worth as compassion instead of in dollars.

"Your partner cannot find that love within himself, and especially he does not feel it from you. You do not want to forgive him. That is always your choice. But understand that your withholding of love stalls not only your progression as a full and realized spiritual being, but also that of the man whom you cannot forgive. He needs your love and understanding to show him the way. In order to truly heal, your partner has to forgive himself. He needs to see that you can forgive him, so he can forgive himself. Forgiveness is the vehicle used to correct misunderstanding and to help let go of fear. Forgiveness is love in action.

"As you sit here, you feel as though you failed him. When you made an agreement in spirit, you promised that you would help him to resist the lure of earthly trappings, but his memory of lust and greed overtook him and he fell short. You have not failed. You were able to give this man only as much love as he felt worthy of receiving from you. You both have worked on this before, and you will do so again. You have each progressed, and you will progress further, but only through love. You must now release him to his own wanderings and creations. In the end, he will eventually understand this aspect of his being.

"Your nightmares have been your own sensing of your husband's guilt, denial, and hatred of himself for what he has caused. So many come over here and needlessly bring with them these conditions of the earthly mind. They try and manipulate things and people here the way they did on the earth, only to find it has no effect. No one can control another. The only force that is strong is the power of love. Forgive him so that he can forgive himself. Blessings and peace, dear one. I am always by your side."

The message ended, and I turned to Susan and let out a great sigh. We parted with a hug and the promise to keep in touch.

UPDATE

Bobby's murderer was captured. Dan, the other woman's lover, was found in Mexico, as Bobby had relayed in his message to Susan. Susan has taken her guide's words of wisdom to heart. She has forgiven her husband and herself, and continues the process of expressing her feelings. She has begun to see her friends, and even dated a few times. As she said to me on the phone, "My life is in order for the first time. I miss Bobby,

but I also know that we will be together again. In the meantime, I have a lot to be thankful for, and I am so glad to know
that I have a guardian angel who loves me enough to keep me
on a spiritual path."

When Someone Is Murdered

When someone we love is senselessly murdered, the surviving family members and friends are usually angry, bitter, and
full of blame, as Susan was. All these feelings are part of the
grieving. It is understandable. Anger turns into guilt, as there
are always so many who believe that there was something they
could have done to prevent such a crime. If there is a trial,
then the grieving is continually stirred up as the evidence is
presented and witnesses testify. This is a horrendous period of
life for all those involved. On one hand, you want the trial to
be over so you can have some closure; on the other hand, you
want to make sure that justice is served and everything is done
properly. Not only is murder shocking, but often the surviving
family members and friends are tormented by thoughts of their
loved one's last minutes on earth.

When someone is thrown out of the physical body suddenly, as in a violent death, the spirit may not know for a while
that it has passed over. It may wander around the earth realm
as if in a dream. It also may become agitated and restless once
it realizes that it is no longer alive in the physical body. Sometimes these souls become lost and bound to earth. However,
once a soul has made the adjustment to the spiritual level, a
relative or spirit guide is there to assist it. The communication
I have had with murder victims has been a mixture of confusion on the one hand, and concern for the living on the other.

There are many reasons why murder occurs. First of all, it
may be due to a karmic debt that has to be repaid. Second, the

consciousness of a killer may be at such a base level that there is no spiritual awareness present. So he thinks nothing of committing murder. Third, someone may choose to deliberately interfere with another's life's direction, and murder is the result. Grieving for a murdered person may be a very difficult process. Be patient, as it will take some time. Remember that forgiveness can help you get through your own painful feelings.

FRIENDS

We often hear the expression: we are born into a family, but we choose our friends. Actually, we choose both family and friends, as hard as that may be to believe. All have traveled through the seas of time with us. Even friends that we knew only part of our lives, perhaps in our youth, and no longer contact, have been with us before and probably will be again. Friends, like family, are part of our soul group and are truly kindred spirits. We count on our friends to be on call through good times and bad, and especially when we grieve.

A friend is someone in whom we can completely confide. We know that he or she has our best interest at heart and will take the time to listen and assist us. A friend will provide encouragement and guidance when needed. Friendship is indeed one of life's most treasured gifts.

Losing a close friend is like losing an arm, and our despair can cut deeper than a knife. We don't expect our friends to die; we think they will always be at our side. So when a friend dies, it seems as though our lifeline is gone. We reflect upon our lives. We dwell in memories of the past. We wonder about our future without our friend nearby. The death of a friend may be so unthinkable that we immediately begin to reevaluate our lives and own mortality. Remember that we have chosen to learn from our relationship with our friends. Mostly, we have had many opportunities to love and serve because of it.

I lost a good friend a while back, and it was such a shock for me. I couldn't believe he was gone. We had shared so many experiences together that I thought our friendship would last forever. When he became ill, I was devastated, but I stood by his side until the end. Soon after, he came to me in spirit. It was consoling to know that he wasn't lost, and that he was all right. I think we all want to know that our friends are still okay wherever they are.

I want to relate the following that occurred on a flight from New York to Los Angeles. It speaks of the true meaning of friendship. I had just settled into my seat, and looked over to the person next to me. It was a lady about fifty years old with flaming red hair and a very well made-up face. She nodded hello and introduced herself as Ruby.

"Are you the man on television who talks to the dead?"

"Yes," I replied.

Ruby said something about a person named Lillie putting me in the seat next to her. Not sure what she meant, I just smiled.

"I am on my way home from Lillie's funeral. She was my best friend."

I resigned myself to listening to Ruby, feeling that she needed to talk. Little did I know it was going to be the best five hours I had ever spent on a plane.

Ruby told me how she and her friend Lillie met some thirty-odd years ago. That seemed to be the start of a long and beautiful friendship between the two.

"We both loved to sew," said Ruby. "Lillie was an avid cloth doll maker, and I assisted her by making dresses for all the dolls. We made close to two hundred dolls and gave them away to little girls in hospitals. Lillie often said that the dolls would cheer up the girls and help them to get better."

Ruby said that she and Lillie were inseparable, and people assumed they were sisters. They were married within a month of one another, and each to a man named Paul. She told me how she and Lillie went through life, helping each other through the hard times and sharing their delight in the good times.

Then she said, "I was there when she was diagnosed with leukemia, and we cried together. I hoped against hope that she could lick it, but we both knew it wasn't meant to be. I was there every day in the hospital to hold her hand before she died."

I asked, "How are you going to get through life without your friend?"

To which Ruby emphatically replied, "I am going to do something which I think Lillie would have liked. I am going to repair those old, worn-out dolls we made a long time ago, and give them to children who need them."

Then she said, "I often dream of Lillie. I feel her around me, too. I ask her for guidance when I need it. It's reassuring to know that I can be with her in that way, but I still miss seeing her in the flesh."

The plane landed, and I bade Ruby good-bye and good luck. I thought, *How beautiful of Ruby to carry on in her friend's memory*.

I sat in my seat while everyone rushed past to get off. When I realized I was the last one left, I grabbed my bag and walked toward the front of the plane. As I made my way past several aisles, I happened to spot, in front of a seat on the floor, a little doll probably forgotten by its owner. Thinking it an odd coincidence, I picked up the doll and looked at it. I gasped out loud. Both of its eyes were gone, but its smile remained intact.

I looked up. I knew that I had just been given a gift from spirit, and wondered if it was Lillie. It was a gentle reminder of the enduring love of two friends.

HEALING GUIDELINES

- Allow yourself to go through the complete grieving process.
- Communicate your feelings to friends or other members of the family. Never hold back your feelings, thinking that you have to be in control. If it is difficult to speak with people you know, perhaps a therapist or support group would be the best outlet to express your inner feelings and thoughts.
- Take one day at a time. Do not feel you must accomplish everything at once, including the household chores. Ask for a friend's help to manage the practical tasks. Simple chores like paying bills, household repairs, and grocery shopping can be overwhelming. Don't be afraid to ask for help.
- Be patient and gentle with yourself. Your grief will be sporadic. Some days you will feel okay; other days you will sit and stare into space, feeling numb and alone.
- It is normal to burst out occasionally in fits of anger. Let it out, but don't harm yourself or anyone else.
- If your children are young, talk to them about the loss. They, too, are suffering and grieving. Encourage them to communicate their feelings as well. Let them know that they are not alone, that you are in this together and to-

gether you will get through it. Assure them that you are still going to be with them and that you will not leave.

- Let your children comfort you if they choose. This could be a wonderful way of healing both of you.

- As time goes by, make some effort to keep in touch socially. Don't isolate yourself. Get out to a movie or a dinner with friends.

- Nurture yourself. This may mean puttering around in your garden, or buying some plants for your home.

- You may want to get a pet from the local shelter. Often, when we preoccupy ourselves with others, including pets, we don't dwell on the past. Pets are perfect company and will comfort you with unconditional love.

- Begin a journal and write about your loved one, whether it is your partner or friend. You may want to remember certain events that were meaningful, or write about your feelings on a day-to-day basis.

- Acknowledge yourself and what you have been through. Evaluate your strengths and weaknesses. Can your experiences help others? In time you may want to reach out and help others through their grief process.

- Don't jump into other relationships prematurely. This may be your way of masking your pain and sorrow. Give yourself space. When you are ready, you'll know.

- See this experience as an opportunity to open yourself to your spiritual life.

- Leave the door open to love again. You are not hurting or betraying anyone. Your partner is in spirit. He or she would only want your complete happiness.

5

TOO YOUNG TO DIE

*E*ach of us comes back upon the shores of this earth for a very distinct purpose. When that purpose is accomplished, we leave. Some of us are here to experience a long life, while other souls need only a brief experience before returning to their spiritual homes in heaven. The choice is made before incarnating into our physical bodies. When we can look at life from this perspective, and acknowledge that time and space are earthly dimensions, and that we are eternal beings, we can begin to understand the nature of life and death in a much clearer light.

The death of a child is perhaps the ultimate loss for a person to endure. How can anyone be prepared for the shock of losing a son or a daughter, or a grandson or a granddaughter? Ask any parent, and he or she would probably say, "I could never survive it," or "I'd never be the same," or "I'd be completely destroyed for the rest of my life." Nothing can ever come close to the indescribable pain one experiences at a child's death, or of the hopelessness that follows. And though parents usually do survive, the loss changes them forever.

When a child dies, parents have to face the incomprehensible: *my child shouldn't die before me*. They suffer enormous guilt because they feel responsible for the death in some way. *What should I have done to prevent this?* They feel worthless, inadequate, and powerless because they believe they have defaulted on their parental obligations. Instead of seeing themselves as parents, they become *parents of their dead children*. There is no clearheaded thinking for such parents. No matter how much protection and caring a parent gives a child, he or she always feels responsible in some way. Besides the sense that a child died before his or her time, the death always seems to be unnatural, and ultimately parents believe that somehow they are to blame.

 ## THE CHILD—PARENT CONNECTION

The relationship of child to parent is more intimate than any relationship. A child is the fullest expression of a parent's love. Our children are born as extensions of ourselves. A new parent prepares for the coming birth of her baby, fostering its health and growth in the womb, and escorting the new life into the world. We become watchful eyes for the child, shielding and protecting him from anything that may threaten or potentially bring harm. We count on our children to continue into future generations long after we are gone; they give us hope and immortality.

The child–parent connection has so many threads on so many levels that the ties go beyond biological, emotional, and mental understanding. After all, this connection originates at a soul level, at which point each one makes a decision to be with the other. Therefore, there is a prearranged agreement between the incoming soul and the parents. Based on my experience, I have found that many of these arrangements involve much needed growth in the areas of self-love and self-forgiveness. Sometimes a child is helping a parent learn to love no matter what. Sometimes a parent decides to go through a certain situation, such as the death of a child, so he can help another person at a later date. Whatever the reasons, the experiences are all lessons of a soul nature.

As I have discussed in my books, *Talking to Heaven* and *Reaching to Heaven*, each one of us is on a spiritual journey. We are individual sparks of light, a part of the one great light or God Force energy. Each soul has its individual path to follow in which to learn about its divine self. Therefore, when a child leaves the physical world prematurely, it is a decision of the soul. Sometimes a soul will not even complete the entire birth process. Many times souls leave in horrendous and inexplicable ways. The important thing to always keep in mind is that *there is no death*. Parents will be with their child again, just as they have been many lifetimes before. Remember that the spirit of a child is alive in a *mental* spiritual world and is always aware of its parents' thoughts and feelings.

PRENATAL DEATH

On the physical level, a woman's pregnancy represents a hope and a dream. She merges with her mate to create a new life. An expecting mother feels a special link with her unborn child that is known only to her. Although a father is also connected to the new life, it is truly the mother who has a unique bond with the newly forming life. Everything a mother feels, thinks, says, and dreams is somehow communicated on a spiritual level to the being growing inside her. An expectant mom has many high hopes as well as many concerns for her unborn child.

When a death occurs before birth, as in miscarriage, a mother-to-be feels not only cheated of her dream, but also feels at fault, as if she were directly responsible for the death. After all, the baby died inside her body, and she blames herself for not being a safe receptacle for her unborn child. Her grieving can involve excessive self-criticism and utter remorse. In the most severe of prenatal deaths, a few women may even feel like murderers. At the very least, a woman feels unimaginable inner conflict and turmoil and tremendous grief. Of course, a father feels disturbed, too. He may blame himself for not taking better care of mother and baby in some way.

When a baby dies prematurely, parents feel that they have been denied the privilege of raising a child and having a legacy. To add to the tragedy of the situation, parents have to face the embarrassment of their family and friends. So often those around the parents think such a loss is immaterial because a baby was never born, and therefore a life was never lived. Even the medical community may callously dismiss a prenatal death too quickly. How insensitive to tell a mother-to-be that a part of her is dead, but that it doesn't matter, she can try again. I feel we need to acknowledge that any prenatal death is extremely painful for the parents.

In many cases, the trauma of miscarriage, or prenatal complications ending in death, affect a woman's confidence about future pregnancies. She may not necessarily trust herself to competently carry another child. She is vulnerable to the worry of losing a baby again. Hopefully, a woman can come to an understanding and complete acceptance of the situation. She has to feel healthy and confident physically, as well as emotionally, before taking on the experience again.

From a spiritual point of view, I have been told that this is not only a lesson for the mother, but also that this may be nature's way of forming more durable and stable energies in a woman's body for a future inhabitant. In other words, what happens on a physical level may just be an end result of work being done on a spiritual or etheric level.

In the case of any prenatal death, parents must first recognize that they are grieving. The parents' feelings of shock and guilt may last longer than anticipated or expected. They may think that they are not meant to be parents, and the experience can scare them out of having children in the future.

Abortion, on the other hand, comes with its own unique array of heated social and political problems that add to the guilt and remorse a woman feels. To me, a political stand on abortion is completely irrelevant. It is a spiritual matter. A woman feels the same feelings about an abortion as she does about a miscarriage, plus the added self-condemnation. The fact that there is a strong desire by many to label her as a murderer only adds salt to the wound. Often a woman may not understand that she is in fact grieving. Depending upon her own beliefs, the loss may throw her into a depression that lasts for years.

Whatever the reason for having an abortion, the lesson is always about love, acceptance, and self-worth for the woman.

I cannot tell you how many times spirits have communicated that a soul is *not* destroyed by abortion, because it does not fully inhabit the forming embryo. A soul knows about the upcoming abortion, and when it occurs, it returns to the higher spiritual levels to prepare for the next available vehicle, one more suited to carry it through to life.

I have been with many women who live in shame, self-denial, and fear because of the social stigma of abortion. In some cases, lives are literally ruined. Whenever a woman goes through an abortion, whether she admits it or not, she is grieving a loss. I always recommend that she seek proper counseling so that she can discuss her feelings in a safe environment. Too many women suffer a lifetime, even lifetimes, of pain, and it doesn't have to be that way. Instead of condemning women, perhaps society can help them to understand the responsibilities of bringing forth life into a world. We must also realize that *God makes no mistakes*. Every experience has a reason, and all experiences are for our spiritual growth.

 ## SUDDEN INFANT DEATH SYNDROME (SIDS)

Another premature death of a child is SIDS, also known as crib death, which occurs during the first year of life. Unfortunately, there are no warning signs for this tragedy. In the United States alone SIDS is the cause for eight to ten thousand deaths a year. Most of these deaths have been known to occur between midnight and nine o'clock in the morning, and a possible reason for the death is the actual physical position of the baby. Up to now medical science has revealed little else to aid in the understanding of SIDS.

When I was about ten, my best friend Scott's mom was having a baby. At the time, Connie was the first pregnant lady I had every seen. One afternoon Scott and I ended our regular football practice, and we stood on a trestle overlooking the on-coming cars, waiting for Scott's parents to pick us up. When they arrived in their old Buick, I had one of my intuitive ex-periences. From my angle overhead, I could see right through the windshield into the front seat. I distinctly remember look-ing at his mother's pregnant tummy. Till this day I remember the leopard-print dress she was wearing. When I looked at her belly, I had this very strange and sickly feeling that made me think something was not right in there.

A month later, the baby was born healthy and normal. By then I had forgotten all about my feeling that day on the over-pass. However, two weeks after the birth, I called Scott, and his father answered the telephone. He told me, "The baby died." In a state of shock, I dropped the receiver and let out a cry. That was the first time I had ever heard of a baby dying. It was unfathomable to me. Then that uncomfortable feeling I had came back. Deep down, I hoped I hadn't been the cause of anything. I asked my mother if I could go over to Scott's house to help in some way, but she said, "Now is not the time." I re-member going into my backyard and looking over the fence at Scott's house. A black truck was parked out front with the words CITY MORGUE. I knew that it was there to pick up the dead baby's body, and I immediately ran back into my bed-room, lay on the bed, and cried.

When I saw Scott's mother several days later, she looked terrible. I could tell that she had been crying, and I could tell in kind of a weird way that she blamed herself for the baby's death. I couldn't tell her about my feeling that day at football practice. I didn't understand it myself. I was just grateful for my mother's reassuring words, "It's in God's hands."

When an infant dies within the first few months of life, the bond that has already been formed between parent and child is suddenly severed. If an infant dies in a hospital, a parent has to return home and face an empty nursery. In the case of SIDS, a child is at home when he or she dies, and the parents face their child's death all alone. There are no warnings. One minute the child is healthy, the next moment there is no movement. The shock and disbelief are enormous. Sometimes this situation causes a parent to deny that the baby has in fact died. They search desperately for an answer, a reason for the baby's death, and cannot find one. Besides having to face inquiries from doctors and others about the cause of death, a parent continues to question, *What did I do wrong? What could have I done to prevent this?* After the funeral, parents must face the final tasks of putting away infant clothes, toys, bottles, and other belongings. Feelings of emptiness and loneliness set in, especially for a mother. Looking at other pregnant women, or mothers with their infant babies, may trigger the loss over and over again without warning. These feelings may recur many years after the death of her baby.

GRIEVING THE LOSS

Grieving parents are very different from other grieving persons. The death of their child represents loss on so many levels, including the loss of dreams and aspirations for their children. When a child dies, these goals and desires fall into a bottomless void of empty promises and dead ends. Subsequently, parents live their lives with a lot of could-haves and what-ifs. Even as they go through the grieving process and begin to heal their wounds, the hole is never sealed completely.

So many parents who come to me are angry with God for

taking their child. They see the death as a form of punishment and wonder how could a loving God do such a thing. I have heard them curse at God and the Universe. I can only share and express with parents what I have learned through my work in the spirit world, and that is, there is no such thing as a vengeful or punishing God.

Each parent must begin the road to healing by actually going through the phases of the grief process beginning with shock, denial, and anger. Often parents are angry with everyone, including friends, family, and the medical community. They look at other people's children and can't understand why these children are still alive and theirs are not. One day they feel they can do something; the next day they are in deepest despair. Many grieving parents try to rush through the process, thinking that it won't hurt as much, but they are only prolonging the agony and suffering.

Grieving the loss of a child is a heart-wrenching process. Patience is essential. You have to take as much time as necessary. There is no time line to follow, no calendar to help mark off the pain. Everyone heals in different ways, and at a different pace. Part of this healing depends upon three things: first, a parent's relationship with his and her child; second, a parent's state of physical and mental health; and third, the support system of relatives, friends, neighbors, and others.

When a child dies, the hardest thing for parents to do is to talk about it, but it is important that they express their feelings. A father especially may have the greatest difficulty in discussing his experience and may not even display any sense of loss. He, too, needs to be encouraged to express his feelings. If either parent's feelings are buried and repressed for an extensive period of time, the results often lead to the break-up of marriage, and other unhealthy forms of unexpressed grief.

In time each parent may recognize that the intensity of the

child's death may subside. However, no matter how busy they keep themselves, parents never get over the death, but rather find ways to survive it. The following stories are from parents whose children have died. In their own words, they have described their personal grief, sharing how the dreams they had for their children were painfully extinguished. Some have gone on with their lives and have helped others in the same situation. Others have gone deep inside themselves and have found an inner spiritual strength that they never knew they had. These parents tell that they now have a stronger connection to the Universal source and how the relationship with their child gave them an opportunity to learn about love. I have chosen these individuals to demonstrate that even in the worst of tragedies, one can find an opportunity for incredible growth. It is my deepest desire that parents feel some grain of peacefulness amidst their sorrow, and know that their lives were blessed by the beautiful soul known as their son or daughter for however long he or she inhabited earth.

 ## THERE ARE NO ACCIDENTS

The following story is from a very beautiful woman named Joerdie, whose son died in an explosion and fire in his own house. Joerdie and her husband Eric attended one of my demonstrations aboard a cruise that Dr. Brian Weiss and I conducted in the Mediterranean several years ago. This is her description of the experience she and her family endured.

> I can barely remember what life was like before December 17, 1997. It seems that life before was a blur, and life now is clearer and filled with more light and

love. The sudden passing of our son changed the lives of many people—his father and myself, his brother, his wife and daughter, and others who loved him, and also many who never met him. When Ian crossed over to the spirit world, he opened doors for us to discover and experience the eternal life of the spirit. He helped us to remember that we are indeed spiritual beings having a human experience.

The night before Ian passed over, a dear friend of mine came to me in a dream. She was dressed all in white and told me to meditate on three things upon waking: (1) Death is never an accident. (2) There are no coincidences. (3) Only love is real. The next morning, I told my husband about the dream and how peaceful my sleep had been. It was that very evening when the emergency room physician told us that Ian's injuries had taken his life. I knew then that Ian wasn't really gone. Instead, I felt that Ian's spirit was released to a place of love and peace. I knew he was better than he had been since coming into this incarnation.

The day after the explosion and fire that took Ian's life, my younger son Scott said he felt that our studying Dr. Brian Weiss's books and tapes was the Universe helping us to prepare for Ian's passing. Unfortunately, Eric had not had that advantage. A couple of weeks before, Scott and I had watched James Van Praagh on *The Larry King Show*, and I had ordered his book, *Talking to Heaven*. The book was waiting for us when we returned from Ian's memorial service. To me it was another gift from the Universe. Scott and I read and reread the book; we were so helped by the healing information. I so hoped that my husband would read the book, and I was so happy when he did. It was the beginning of his spiritual awakening.

When we found out that James and Dr. Brian

Weiss were doing workshops aboard a Mediterranean cruise, Eric and I decided to take part. It was a life-changing trip.

Before the start of James's workshop, something curious happened. I was sitting in the auditorium along with hundreds of others. I looked down and found a photo of Ian in my lap. It had been in my wallet, but I don't remember taking my wallet out of my purse. It was a class photo of Ian from grade school. He was wearing a T-shirt with a hole in it. I remember asking Ian all those years ago, "Why couldn't you have worn a better shirt for your school picture?" No one on the ship except Eric and I had ever seen that photo.

During the workshop, we listened to James talk about life after death, and I knew that we had come to the right place. Then James began his readings from spirit. We were many rows back in a large auditorium filled with hundreds of people, and James relayed several messages to people in the audience. Then he said something completely amazing.

"I have a young man here who is showing me a T-shirt with a hole in it. Does this make sense to anyone in the room?"

At first I didn't know what to do. Then I stood up. I thought to myself, *Now I understand why he wore that old shirt.*

James came down the aisle toward us. "This young man is giving me a pearl necklace. Do you understand?"

I couldn't believe what he was saying, and yet I completely understood. In a dream the night before, Ian came to me and said he was giving me pearls of wisdom to make a beautiful necklace. That very morning I had noted it in my journal.

"Is this your son?"

I nodded yes, and tears began to well up in my eyes.

"Your son is showing me notes, musical notes, and a guitar. He is playing a guitar."

I responded, "Yes." Ian had played guitar in a band for years.

James continued. "I feel that your son's passing was sudden. There is an explosion and then fire." Then he paused a moment. "He is telling me that he was afraid of dying in a fire."

I told James, "Ian was always scared to death of fire."

"Your son was psychic. He had a premonition about his death."

James then said, "I must say that Ian was both a devil and an angel."

Ian was certainly that.

James seemed to be listening to the silence in the room before he spoke again. "He is telling me that he had to leave his life early for his spiritual growth and evolution. Do you understand what I mean?"

I nodded that I did.

"He is also telling me that you are a medium, and that you can contact the spirit world yourself. He is saying you need to pay more attention and listen."

James shared so much information that only Ian could have given him, but this last statement came as a complete surprise. I had been dreaming of Ian, and speaking to him in my dreams, but I never thought of myself as a medium.

Then James said, "Your son is very happy and peaceful, and he wants you to be happy once again, too. He is saying, I wish you could see how beautiful it is where I am now!"

Two nights after James's reading, I began to receive messages from Ian and a man named Glenn, who told me that he had passed over one week after Ian. I did not know Glenn, but I had just met his sister Joan on board the cruise. Joan told me that she thought Glenn and Ian sounded like they could have been friends, and verified all the information Glenn gave to me. We realized that Ian and Glenn were good friends in the spirit world and had spent many lifetimes together. From then on, Ian and Glenn began to visit me regularly.

Those healing words from our son through James gave Eric and me a sense of calm and renewal. Our lives were forever changed. We were able to view what formerly looked like problems as opportunities for spiritual development. My husband began to approach his medical practice and all of his life in a more spiritual way. We are now able to see Ian's passing as a beautiful gift. By learning not to fear death, we no longer fear life. The illusion of having control over circumstances gave way to the love and wisdom of the Universe. Getting in touch with the God spark within has helped us to help others, and that help has been passed along to even more people. Of course, we miss our son Ian, but his spirit is with us all of the time. We can talk to him whenever we need to on the free line.

UPDATE

Joerdie told me, "Before Ian's death, you might say I lived an unenlightened life. I worried about everything, and had a lot of judgment about people and situations. I was always afraid of not having enough. I lived by rote, and I was not very sensitive to what was really important." After her son's death, and through her process of grief, Joerdie has changed her perspective on life. As she said, "I now have a relationship with God that is built on understanding and unconditional love for *all* of life. The more the Universe reveals to me about our past lives, the more this present life makes sense to me. I have found out through my communication with Ian that he had committed suicide in his immediate past life, and had returned to this one to complete the rest of that lifetime. Ian had written about suicide when he was fifteen, which was the age in his past life that he committed suicide. He said that he was being sexually abused and couldn't take it anymore. The day after his passing, I learned that he had been sexually abused in this life. I was shocked and angry. But Ian was able to turn the experience around in this life by having compassion for homeless kids and adults." Joerdie finished her conversation by adding that she continues to learn from her son in spirit. "He is always teaching me about love and compassion."

 ## A TELEPHONE CALL TO HEAVEN

I have seen the trauma and devastation of a child's death on the parents, but the loss also has a disturbing effect on the whole family, as you will see in this next tragic story. Fortunately for Bill and Donna, and their children Ryan and Keri, the tragedy of young Chris's death has brought them even closer together. Donna's poignant and painful recounting of her experience has helped to heal others facing the same heartache.

> Our nightmare began when my husband Bill and I were startled by the doorbell at four in the morning. We jumped out of bed, our hearts pounding as we made our way to the door. When we opened it, we experienced every parent's nightmare. Two grim-faced

policemen stood in the doorway. We knew the news was not good. My legs grew weak as they proceeded to tell us that our son Christopher had been in a serious car accident a block away from our house. It appeared that he had fallen asleep at the wheel, run off the road, and hit a tree. The ambulance had taken him to the emergency room of our local hospital. My mind reeled, and my stomach ached, as I rushed to throw on some clothes. As I ran out of the house, I instinctively reached for my rosary beads, which were resting on my nightstand. In the car I began to pray, "Oh God, how could this be happening? Please take care of my son. Please don't let him die—not my baby. Jesus, help him." Bill thought he would be all right. "After all," he said, "accidents happen all the time, and most people are fine." I don't know how Bill was able to drive; he seemed so out of it.

We speculated on what must have happened. Chris and a few of his friends had gone to Magic Mountain the day before to celebrate their high school gradua- tion, which was to take place the following week. He arrived home around dinnertime and told us how much fun he had had and recounted some of the funny incidents that had happened. It had to have been a tiring day, but Chris was always full of energy and on the go, so I wasn't surprised when he told us that he was going over to a friend's house to hang out for a while after dinner. The last words I said to him were, "Don't be late; you have school tomorrow." He kissed us good-bye, as he always did, and said, "I know. Don't worry." We were pretty sure he would have a few beers at his friend's, and because of the hour, it could have been a mixture of alcohol and fatigue that caused him to fall asleep at the wheel. We were sure that the damp and foggy morning could have tired him even more.

He was so close to home, only a block away, the po-
liceman said. If only he could have stayed awake a few
minutes longer. He hardly ever came home that time
of the morning because he knew he would be in trouble. I berated myself for not waking up when he wasn't
home by midnight and paging him. He was always so
good about calling me back.

We ran into the hospital in a panic and were told
that the doctors were working on Chris and would
talk to us soon. So we began the agonizing wait. The
reality was setting in; we prayed like never before. I
don't know how many times I repeated the rosary. Finally the doctor appeared. His face was colorless; he
looked exhausted. I knew what he was going to say before he said it. "Chris had a terrible blow to his head.
There were chest injuries, and we could not stop the
bleeding. He fought hard. We fought hard." But nevertheless our son didn't make it. "I'm so sorry," the
doctor said. I will never forget those words. The pain
of that moment was indescribable. In remembering it
now, I can't believe I didn't literally die from it. Bill
and I collapsed in each other's arms in a state of shock.
The doctor then asked if we would like to see our son.
Bill said he didn't think he could, but I emphatically
said yes. I was there when Chris came into this world,
and I needed to be with him as he left it. I have heard
that our brain releases a chemical at times of great
stress to anesthetize our emotions and protect us from
pain. Well, the chemical had set in, and I felt like a
zombie walking through a world that had stopped. I
sat with my son's body, holding his hand and stroking
his beautiful face, a face I knew I would never see
again in this lifetime. I thought about the day he was
born, and that there was no future for him. He would
always remain eighteen years old in my mind. I wanted

to take in every detail of his face, hands, chest, feet, lest I forget. I looked at his crooked bottom teeth and thought about the retainer we had just ordered. I looked at the little mole above his eyebrow that he had wanted to have removed. How could his life be over?

Bill had changed his mind and entered the room. I had never seen him in so much anguish. His face was almost unrecognizable to me. He just stood there in a trance. Chris and he were so close, and so much alike, I didn't know how he would ever recover from the loss of his son.

As we left the hospital, the sun was shining, and people were beginning their day like any other ordinary one. Bill and I mechanically got into the car and began the drive home, to a life that would never be the same—a life without our youngest child. I said to Bill, "I don't know how we are going to go on without Chris."

Bill had made several calls to our family and friends from the hospital. They would soon be arriving at our home. We would have to start planning the funeral, a task that seemed impossible in our state of mind. Worst of all, we would have to tell our two older children, Keri and Ryan, that their brother died. We were and are a close family, and I knew they would be as devastated as we were. Giving them the details was excruciating for us. Keri just cried and cried in disbelief, and Ryan shouted out, "No, no, not Chris," while he pounded his bed.

The days that followed were surreal. I thank God that we had the love and support of our friends and family. We all needed each other. Everyone loved Chris, and all suffered greatly. The funeral was beautiful. The church was filled with so many people; it was especially comforting to see so many of Chris's friends.

People told us that they would always remember Chris's smiling face, and his joking around and making them laugh. Some of his friends told us that he had helped them through hard times by giving advice on how to solve their problems. I had no idea he had touched so many people. By the time the reception was over, we were feeling the best we had since that horrible morning four days ago.

However, grief permeated the days ahead, and we began to feel worse then ever. Chris's death was still unbelievable to me. I found myself saying over and over again, "Chris is dead. Chris died." I started counting each day since the accident, and each day was harder than the day before. It was one more day since I had last seen my boy. I kept thinking that one day it would be forty or seventy or a hundred days, and then the days would turn into years. I didn't think I could stand it.

It was so quiet around the house with Chris gone. When he was home, there was always the noise of his talking, laughing, singing, and fooling around, telephone calls, and, of course, his favorite reggae music. Keri and Ryan together never made as much noise as Chris. How could one child make such a difference? Every time I did something for the last time, like washing the last of his dirty clothes, changing the last sheets he used, straightening out his room, and canceling his last dental appointment, I was crushed. Everyone talked about *memories*, and the word just made me shudder. I hated that word because all I had left *were* memories. But memories of Chris's eighteen years were hardly enough to last me a lifetime. I started writing down everything about him for fear that I would forget someday.

Bill had to go back to work, but he was operating

on automatic pilot. He had trouble focusing and making decisions. He would come home looking beat up and exhausted. I felt so sorry for him and wished I could comfort him, but I had nothing to give. I just didn't have the strength. Keri and Ryan went back to their classes and were also finding it difficult to function. I am thankful that they had their good friends around them.

I spent days just sitting and thinking and going over all the details concerning Chris's death. I needed to find answers to my questions. *Did he have any pain? Was he conscious at the end? Did he cry out for me?* And the philosophical ones: *Was it his time to die? Would he have died some other way if he had stayed home that night, or was it meant to be?* Ryan said something bizarre after the funeral. He said that Chris told him that he had a vision of his funeral while staring at the carpet in his room a week or so before the accident. He said that he saw his casket, the flowers, and people crying. I thought, *What is that about? Did Chris have some premonition of his death?*

I had trouble praying. I felt abandoned by God. But my mind thankfully contradicted my feelings, and I knew God was with me. Emotionally, I just felt alone. I had always prayed for the health and safety of my family every day. *Why didn't it work this time?* In the hospital Bill and I had prayed the most we ever had, but our prayers hadn't been answered. As a Catholic, I have always believed in eternal life with God in heaven. My faith sustained me when my mother died and also when my grandparents died. But Chris's death was different. Faith alone wasn't enough. I needed to know for sure that my son was in heaven. I needed to know if he was all right and happy, and if he was with people he knew. I wanted to know if he heard me when I talked to him. I wanted to know if he was near us in the house. *Was he the one flicking the lights at odd times? Was he making the electric garage door go up and down by itself?* When we sensed his presence, I wondered, *Are you really here?*

Even though I felt empty, I still prayed. I prayed that God was taking care of him. I prayed that God would let Chris give us signs that he was near. I believed that God had Chris forever, and I prayed that in His mercy, He would grant my requests.

I spent my days reading books on grief, angels, near-death experiences and after-death communication. They were helpful, for knowledge is cathartic. Some months after Chris's death, I saw a television program called *The Other Side* in which a spiritual medium named James Van Praagh explained about his gift to communicate with the dead. I had read about this phenomenon, but to actually see it demonstrated was amazing. The details that came through in the readings for the guests on the show were proof enough for me that James was indeed communicating with spirits. James appeared on several of the segments over the following months. I taped them all, and Bill, Keri, Ryan, and I watched them together. Those shows gave us such hope. We decided that we would try to get in touch with James for our own personal reading.

We soon learned from a radio announcement that James was giving a demonstration in Los Angeles. Bill and I attended. There were about two hundred people in the audience, and it turned out to be an overwhelming experience. The people for whom James did a short reading were randomly chosen, and the messages they received from their deceased loved ones brought them hope, love, and healing. Again, the evidential details of the messages gave absolute validation that people were in communication with their loved ones.

After the demonstration, we immediately called to set up an appointment. James was completely booked well into the next year, but it didn't matter, we would wait. Some time went by, and we received a call from James's office that there had been a cancellation. The next day the four of us arrived for our appointment with a mixture of emotions. We were excited and nervous all at the same time. Bill and I had been praying that Chris would come through clearly and communicate with us. James met us at the door and immediately put us at ease with his endearing personality and kind words. He invited us to sit down, said a prayer, and began the reading.

"Your mother was there and helped him cross over. She is with him."

James continued. "You call him Chris, not Christopher?"

I nodded, "That's right."

James continued. "Okay, let me bring him through for you. I have to tell you something here. Your mother is funny. She is leaning over to him and telling him to be serious about this. She says don't crack up. Don't mess this up; they take it seriously."

We all let out a nervous laugh. Then James continued.

"Chris likes to play around. He's a practical joker and likes to be the center of attention. He is saying, they came here for me. He is a wiseacre. I mean, he is really funny. He wants to goof around. Grandma is shaking her head like some things never change!"

"Exactly," I said.

"Who was looking at a map? Were you looking at a map in the car?"

I replied, "Yes, yes. I was looking at a map on the way here."

"Your son was trying to help you out. He is saying Mom always gets lost."

James took a moment before continuing. "Chris has brought some friends that he has met there. Who is Jonathan or John? He is in spirit with Chris and is about nineteen years old. He passed from a drug overdose. You don't know him, but you will meet his parents. Maybe you already have."

I nodded, "No, not yet."

"Was there any trouble with a vehicle, a car or a motorcycle?"

I responded, "Yes."

"Did he slam into something?"

Again, I said yes.

"Was it a tree, please? I'm being shown a tree. Like *boom* into a tree."

"Yes."

"I feel unconscious right away when this happens. Your son was unconscious. I feel that in some respect he was at fault. He had to claim his responsibility for this situation. It taught him a little bit about being responsible and the preciousness of life."

I answered, "Yes, he fell asleep at the wheel. It was very late in the night."

"He is saying he was very lucky to have you as parents because of your understanding of him. He says that love is letting the person be who he is, on his own path, and knowing that you are still there and still love him and letting him grow. He continues to grow on the other side. I feel there was trouble with him. Not intentional. He was always looking for adventure and excitement. He is giving me the impression that you had to lay down rules for him early on. Do you understand?"

I smiled. "Yes that's right."

"He had to stay in his room because he didn't obey the rules, and the more rules you gave him, the worse he became. Because he is a rebel."

We all laughed at the thought of Chris and his rebelliousness.

"He is saying, I'm sorry for being such a pain in the ass and causing you a lot of trouble and grief. He also wants to tell you he is learning about love in the other realm. He loves you guys very much, by the way. He loves you for coming here tonight. He thanks you."

I was so thankful to be there as well.

"Are you doing something with shelves?" James asked.

I let out a laugh. "Yes!"

James laughed along. "He says, God, she's filling up those shelves. He is watching you do that. You are making a nice home for your family, understand? Spirit is with you, understand?"

"Yes, we recently moved, and I'm still putting things away."

Then James turned his attention to my daughter, Keri.

"Did you, or someone, put a rosary in his coffin?"

Keri answered, "My mom did."

"Did you take a rose from his funeral service?"

"Yes!" she answered.

"Did you put it in a box or a Bible?"

"I put it in a box."

"And did you write something to him at the time of his death? Did you write a letter or poem to him, and did you read it at his service, or to yourself?"

Keri answered, "Not at the funeral, but I read it to him by myself."

"But you wrote it, didn't you? It was about how you felt about him."

"Yes that's right," Keri answered in amazement.

"He received the letter, and he loves you for it. You wrote, *I'll always love you.* It touched his heart."

Keri was close to tears when she heard this last comment.

"He sometimes did not show his affection to you. He kept his emotions inside. Understand?"

"Yes, I do," she replied.

"But you really pulled his heartstrings. You really got to him. He said he has been saving up his tears and putting them in a box for all of you. Very loving, very, very loving."

Then James said to Keri, "Do you have a music box or a jewelry box?"

"Yes, a jewelry box."

"Did you just get it?"

Keri laughed, again amazed, "Yes!"

"Guess who it's from? It was really a gift from Chris. Your mom or someone might have given it to you, or you got it yourself, but it was really from him because spirit can impress others to buy things."

Keri said, "I saw this jewelry box in a catalog, and I kept debating whether I should get it or not, and then I finally decided to buy it."

James continued, "He is saying good luck with school. Your brother was very proud of you. He says that you were always serious about school. While he was always goofing off, you were studying hard."

Keri let out a laugh. "That's right!"

Then James asked, "Who had a Volkswagen?"

Ryan answered, "We both did!"

"He's telling me, you tell my brother about the Volkswagen. He'll know what you're talking about."

Ryan said, "Oh, wow!"

James turned to Ryan. "Your brother and you have a special link. I must say that to you. It's as if you don't even have to say things to each other because you know exactly what each other is thinking. He wants you to know that this link goes beyond family. You have had lifetimes of learning together—coming back to this physical world and going through experiences together. You know, it's very much like going to school and taking classes together. There's a love between you and your brother that goes beyond time. Do you understand?"

Ryan nodded yes.

James continued with Ryan. "He's saying to me that you cursed him when he died. He said you were pissed off and freaking out and banging your hands on something like a wall. Do you remember this?"

Ryan answered, "Yes."

James spoke to Ryan softly. "Your brother was mad at himself for the accident, and you were feeling his anger. He is saying it wasn't you, okay? Did he call you Ry?"

"Yes, he did."

"Tell Ry I didn't do this on purpose. Is it possible he was drinking?"

"Yes, earlier."

"I do get a sense he was drinking. This is what he is giving me, and I have to tell you what I get. I feel like it was his own fault, and he takes full responsibility for that. Do you have his cap?"

"Yes, I have several," Ryan answered.

"You don't like to wear it, though?"

"I don't want to ruin them."

"He says, my brother makes them into a shrine. Did he have some trophies?"

I answered this time. "We have them."

"Is there a jacket still around and some T-shirts of his?"

Again I said yes.

"There are certain things you don't want people to touch or have, and he doesn't understand this. He thinks that people should have his things and use them. He is happy that Ryan is wearing some of his shirts."

James asked Ryan, "Do you still need a new car?"

Again, we all laughed in acknowledgment.

"He says he will always love you and will always protect you. He wants you to learn from his stupidity. He said that there was always a feeling with you that you wanted to protect him, but now he will protect you."

James continued, "Ryan, don't go near motorcycles."

Ryan answered, "I love motorcycles. I have two."

"Your brother is saying to be careful on slick ground. Be very careful, you could slide. Only ride on dirt roads, not on the streets. I'm sorry, Ryan, but I have to tell you this."

Ryan said, "I did slip on some water and almost crashed. I do most of my riding in the dirt, though."

"Chris is going to try to help you get a car."

Ryan was happy to hear that. "Good!"

James's attention went to Bill.

"Your son bugs you a lot in your office."

Bill answered, "I know."

"Is his picture on your desk, and have you noticed anything moving or missing?"

"The picture seems to move. I always have to put it back in the morning."

James smiled. "That's Chris bugging you. He says he taps you on the shoulder and tries to rock your chair."

Bill nodded knowingly. "I do feel a poking in my back."

"Also, are the lights flickering on and off?"

"He does that all the time. He started flicking the lights from the beginning and still does it."

James nodded. "He confirms that he is doing that. He says that my dad and I have a good communication going, and he comes in dreams, as well."

"Yes, I have had very vivid dreams of him."

James looked at Bill for a moment. "I see a lot of lavender color around you. Very spiritual. Inspirational. I see spiritual work around you. He says to me that you will be doing some more spiritual work."

Bill nodded. "Yes, I am doing some energy healing for people."

Then James asked, "Did you screw something up with a check or checkbook, because your son is laughing his head off. He says he made you goof."

Bill roared, "Dead on!"

"Do you have an alarm system in your house or office?"

"Yes, both."

"The system recently screwed up."

"Yes, the office security system went off a few days ago, and I had to go over there. It was going off for no reason that I could tell."

"Chris was with you in the car."

We all just sat in amazement as James continued to tell us about our son.

"Do you have a beeper? He says he plays around with the beeper. Did you get beeped and didn't understand the beep?"

Bill let out another laugh. "Yes!"

"Guess who it was!"

Bill shook his head. "Chris would always put his code in when he beeped me. One night we all went out to dinner to celebrate a birthday, and I got a beep. It was Chris's code. I couldn't believe it. It was as if he was telling me that he was there with us."

"He was there! He says don't be such a dad—you can be a kid, too."

Bill's eyes started to fill up with tears.

James continued. "He says he wants you to realize that it's not as painful as you think it is. He is thanking me for helping you. He's having a good time and feeling good. He says he'll come back and do it all over again."

James asked Bill, "Was Chris an altar boy?"

"Yes, he was."

"Do you know a priest who died? Because he has met someone over there, an older gentleman, maybe a pastor or monsignor whom he served as an altar boy."

Bill was dumbfounded. "Yes, Monsignor Gallagher, the pastor of our church, died. Chris served him as an altar boy."

James asked, "Did you have something done with his name or in his name?"

Bill replied, "Yes, we had a memorial set up in his name for scholarships at his school."

"What about a tree? He is telling me something about a tree as a memorial or something."

Again, Bill answered, "Ryan put a cross on the tree that Chris crashed into. People also put flowers there."

James then asked us all, "Okay, do you have any questions?"

Bill jumped in right away. "What does Chris do during a typical day? Does he have a job?"

James replied. "Don't think of their world as night and day because there is no such thing. There is only daylight, no nighttime. They also don't need to eat or sleep, okay? Chris hangs out with kids his own age. He does all the things a kid his age would do. He helps you guys a lot and is learning a lot. Was he in school?"

Bill replied. "Yes, he would have graduated from high school the week after the accident."

James continued. "He says it's hard to explain this to you in some ways, but he is learning different aspects of his soul. He is doing work there that will help him with his soul growth. He is learning about charity right now. He is saying, I help small babies. He loves babies. He helps place babies who cross over. He takes them to people who care for babies. He is saying that he works with young kids who do not realize that they have passed over, kids who die in crashes. Sometimes when people die they are not aware of it right away. He has to do this to balance things out, he says."

Bill asked, "Does it take a lot of energy for him to come here?"

"He says it's different from what you might think. It feels very heavy, but the love that you have for him is the fuel that helps bring him down and enables him to stay here. It's like sitting in a pool of water eight feet deep. Spirits don't need to come down here; it's not their natural world."

James turned his attention to me.

"Did you make a shrine to him after he died with pictures, candles, flowers, or a cross?"

"I have a few pictures in a hutch with a candle and some flowers."

"Did you sit on his bed and think of him a lot and say prayers to him. Were you crying?"

I answered yes.

"He wants you to know that he is safe. So your prayers have been answered. Okay?"

I felt relieved. "Thank you."

Then James said something we never expected.

"Do you guys have a dog that passed, because he is saying he is with a dog. Was it his dog? Because there is something special between him and this dog. He says that he is with him. Is this something you wanted to know, because he says that you wanted to know this."

My eyes opened wide. "Oh, yes! This is unbelievable. Our dog, Brandi, was killed four days before Chris on the same street. We all loved her very much. I hoped and prayed that Chris and Brandi were together. He especially was very close to her. I told Chris that if he mentioned Brandi at this reading, I would know for sure that it was him."

James's face lit up with a big grin. "I love it! Okay, let's end now with a prayer. Thank you, friends, all of you, for your help and assistance in coming through and bringing your messages of love, joy, peace, and reassurance. We thank you, dear guides and helpers also, for all your assistance tonight in transforming the thoughts into messages. We ask you to please help everyone here on their own path of love and light. Thank you and bless you."

The meeting ended with all of us hugging one another. On the way home we all talked about the messages that Chris sent through James. We were elated and filled with such joy and love. It was by far the best day we had had since Chris's death. We couldn't believe the intricate details that were relayed. It proved to us without a doubt that Chris was around us. He did hear us when we talked and prayed to him. He was happy and okay. The reading was like a telephone call to heaven. We couldn't wait to tell our family and friends of our experience.

UPDATE

Donna and I have kept in touch since the family came to see me. She has told me that the family has begun to heal since the reading. As she said, "Our despair gradually disappeared, and our faces had more smiles than tears. We still miss him immensely and always will, but just knowing that he is around us and that we can talk to him is such a comfort. It brought us peace and hope. We know now that it was just our son's body that died that day; his spirit, personality, essence, and soul are alive and well. Chris did not die, he is alive in heaven, and we will be with him again someday."

She said, "I have no more fear of dying. Death is not an end, only a transition to a better place—our home. Knowing this has enhanced my relationship with God and made it stronger. Sometimes God gives us a gift that allows us to actually experience something, or gives us a little kick in the butt, so to speak, to increase our faith. There is everlasting life after death.

"Chris continues to give us signs from time to time in his joking manner—flicking the lights, turning the radio off and on, giving us smells, and moving things."

Bill and Donna signed up for my classes on Psychic Development. Every day they continue to learn more about their own spirituality. Bill has expanded and augmented his energy-healing abilities and helps many people. They share their experience with other people who have lost loved ones in the hope that they will be comforted as they were.

MY ONLY SON

I have been fortunate to share some special moments and to counsel thousands of parents through the organization called The Compassionate Friends, a support group of parents and siblings. No matter how much proof through details that come through in communication, a parent still feels robbed of his or her child. A part of their own lives is lost forever.

Marie narrates this next story. She is one of the parents I have met at The Compassionate Friends organization. I conducted a workshop for them in New York in 1994, and she was a great help in getting it arranged. Her son was killed in an automobile accident the year before, and she has been touching the hearts of many ever since.

It was Saturday, August 7, 1993, another perfect day in sunny California. I was visiting my sister and her family, while my son Peter and my husband were back East. Peter had just graduated from Syracuse University, and he was in New York with my husband Phil, interviewing for jobs in the music publishing business. I had spoken to him the night before, and he was excited about a particular job for which he had a second interview. I assured him, "It's a lock," as I had no doubt that he would land the job.

My sister and I decided to drive down to Carmel to walk around and window-shop. We had to be back in time for a farewell party for my nephew, who was leaving for graduate school the next day. When we returned from Carmel that Saturday afternoon, we were exhausted. We decided to forgo the farewell party, order a pizza, and watch a movie instead. We had just popped the video into the VCR when the phone rang.

It was nine p.m.—midnight in New York. It was Phil. He told me that Peter was dead. I heard myself say, "It's simply not possible." The unknowable—the un-fathomable—had happened. The shock and disbelief of that moment is so indelibly etched in my mind that its scar has shaped all subsequent events of my life.

The night before, Peter went out with a few of his college buddies who were in town for the weekend. The weather had been terrible all day, so by ten p.m. boredom had set in and the prospect of bar hopping held considerable appeal. By two a.m. Peter lay dead on a Manhattan highway. He was killed instantly when the young man who was driving lost control of the car on a rain-slick road. Peter shot out the rear window like a rocket. There were four boys in that car—three were shaken and bruised. My precious son Peter was dead in an instant.

Peter was our only child, and he and I shared a very special kinship. All mothers love their sons, but there was a unique bond between us that most envied. It was as if we could communicate telepathically—complet-ing each other's thoughts and anticipating one an-other's needs. Because we were a family of three, there was always that sort of two-against-one dynamic, and since Peter's sense of humor was fiercer than mine, it was usually the two of us against Phil. Poor Phil never had a chance when Peter and I were on. In my mind and heart, Peter could do no wrong. I was putty in his hands from the time he could crawl, and he knew it. And Peter adored me. In his view I was bigger than life. There was nothing, no problem, that his mom couldn't solve. My life bordered on perfect. And as it goes when something seems too good to be true, it usually is.

I like to believe that Peter defined who I was.

There are many that would argue that this is an unhealthy perspective. But for those who have lost an
only child, it is a deep-seated truth. I don't mean that
my world revolved only around Peter, because I always
had a very full life. I've always been in business, and as
a result of my many affiliations, I've traveled around
the world with many accomplished people. My associ-
ations brought me great personal satisfaction. But
with all the glamour and the glory, my greatest joy was
being Pete's mom. Nurturing him and accompanying
him through life into manhood was the greatest satisfaction of all.

Peter loved me unconditionally, the way a parent
loves a child. This is no small thing. Too often the
love between people is a qualified love. Peter and I
were devoted to each other. I've since heard many bereaved parents try to describe this kind of connection.
Some parent-child relationships transcend simple explanation. With Peter gone, I felt left in a world where
that particular love and acceptance no longer existed.
Although friends and family surrounded me, I was
alone in the universe. Only Peter could have imag-
ined my pain, and that thought only increased my torment. In my mind's eye, I saw us both churning in
agony and unrelenting grief.

Several years before Peter's death, my mother died.
She and I had as close a relationship as I had with Peter. Her health had been failing for a while, and at the
end we had an intense period of several days where we
said so many things to each other. It is rare to get the
opportunity to say good-bye so completely to someone
you love before it's too late. Jokingly, Mom would say
that if there really was an afterlife, she would find a
way to get a message to me. When she died in 1988, I
waited for a sign from her, but none ever came. My sis-

ter, on the other hand, kept telling me that she felt Mom's presence everywhere. It infuriated me to think that my mother had probably decided to spend her eternity in California. She probably figured we said all there was to say, and she was determined to shower the rest of her attention on my sister.

Unlike my mother's, Peter's death brought me face to face with my own death. Death became my total focus. I needed to know everything about it. I was sure I was already dead except that my body had not caught up with the rest of me. The people that mattered to me most in the world were somewhere else, and I wanted to get there as quickly as I could. I began to read everything about death. I would venture out to a bookstore and head directly to the section on death and dying. I started at the top shelf and worked my way down. By the end of the day my mind was reeling. All that I read seemed to validate my growing belief that Peter's life was simply not over. But I had to find out for sure.

During the winter of 1994, just six months after Peter died, my husband and I were spending a quiet weekend at our house on Long Island. *The Joan Rivers Show* was on TV, and the guest was a young psychic who was demonstrating his ability to receive messages from the other side. We sat riveted as he read for several volunteers from the audience, and they appeared to confirm what he said. I knew I had to find this James Van Praagh.

After Peter died, I joined a support group called The Compassionate Friends, which has chapters all around the world. This organization proved to be the lifeline I needed to survive. A few weeks after seeing James on *The Joan Rivers Show*, I overheard a conversation at one of our meetings that James was coming to New York to give a demonstration. He needed some help in finding an appropriate space that would hold upward of a hundred people. I immediately volunteered my services, and thought it was a good opportunity to get a private reading with him.

On June 17, 1994, ten months after Peter's sudden death, I finally got my wish. My long-awaited private reading with James was scheduled for seven o'clock, and I spent that entire day in an intensely heightened state of anticipation. I felt like a youngster getting ready for a first date.

James has a great sense of humor, and so do I. Peter, too, had an irrepressible sense of humor, and it was immediately apparent to James. During the course of our two hours together, James and Peter both seemed to be having a wonderful time. Peter sent message after message, and became more and more present in the process.

As soon as James began the reading, Peter was by my side.

"Your son in here with you, and he has a great sense of humor. He has been waiting to speak to you for a long time. He says that Nana was the first one to meet him, and he spends a lot of time with her."

I thought to myself, *Could it really be Peter?*

"He is telling me you were folding a blanket and tried to get it to stay up on the top shelf of the closet. Do you understand this?"

I replied with astonishment, "Yes."

"He is showing me a hospital now. Were you talking to someone about going to a hospital?"

By now I was impressed with what James was telling me. I had talked to someone about going into the hospital just an hour before my appointment with him.

"I must say your son is very excited, he can't slow down. He is showing me boxes all over the house. He says he was there with you as you packed the boxes, and was watching you wrap all the photos."

I couldn't believe it. I had been packing to get ready to move to our summer house.

James continued. "He is telling me that he misses you very much. He loves you and misses you."

"I miss you, too, honey," was my tearful reply.

"Peter is showing me his room. He says that you haven't changed a thing, and he is happy to see all of his things where he left them. He is showing me a mirror surrounded by words. There is something hanging on the mirror. Do you know what he is talking about?"

"I know there are diplomas by the mirror, but I can't figure out what's hanging on the mirror. I'll have to look when I get home." I was becoming convinced that Peter was with me. *How could anyone know this information?* I thought.

James continued with messages from Peter. "He is telling me there are things that need taking care of in the house. The stack of magazines in the living room— get rid of them, he says. The door with a squeak. Have Daddy fix it. He is telling me that Daddy has to get on with things. Tell him to start fixing stuff around the house."

I loved hearing Peter telling us to get on with life. It was so reassuring that he was watching over us like that.

At one point James began to laugh. I knew it must be Peter for sure. "Were you in Las Vegas?" James asked. "Or Atlantic City?"

"Oh, yes," I said.

"He is showing me slot machines. He is telling me that he was trying to help you win."

"I was in Atlantic City a short while ago playing the slots, but I was losing. Peter was never good at gambling. What made him think he could help me?"

James went on, "He is telling me about baseball caps. He had a lot of them. Now he is showing me all the pictures on the refrigerator. He wants you to put something in the kitchen that makes noise so that you will know when he is around. Do you understand? He has been trying to get your attention with moving things around in the living room. I am seeing the color red. Is the living room red? Does this make any sense?"

"Yes, it makes a lot of sense to me." I thought to myself, *Yes, I shall watch for something that you manage to knock off the shelves in the red living room, Peter. Nice touch, that clue.*

There was a pause. Then James said, "He is showing me a funeral. He was happy to see all his friends there. He loved the poem they read. He knew it was your idea. He was glad that you didn't invite his girl-friend, Laurie or Lauren?"

"Yes, there were many friends, girlfriends, and ex-girlfriends at Peter's graveside weeping."

I was so glad that Peter had been at his own memo-rial service. It was an extraordinary day.

Then James said, "He is saying that he was with you at the podium."

"I thought I saw the air move up when I stood at the podium. I felt he was there."

"He wants you to know that it was he who knocked the bouquet of roses over. It was at the very end of the service. It was his way of saying it's over!"

"I knew it! No one was even near those roses. Then suddenly the whole thing flopped over in one fell swoop as if some unseen hand had simply whacked it. I knew it must have been Peter."

James got a real kick out of that.

By the time our visit ended, I felt I had actually spent the evening with Peter. I went home feeling giddy with a sense of real connection. I knew that Peter was okay. I also knew that it was as important for him to connect with me as it was for me to connect with him. I was convinced. He was okay. He lived. He was somewhere.

When I got home I was more at peace than I had been since that fateful call. I went into his room to check the mirror and found the tassels from all of Peter's graduation caps—junior high, high school, and college—hanging from it. Then I sat down and wrote Peter a letter.

Dear Peter:

I went to see James Van Praagh tonight. Because I am always compelled to record my thoughts (all of which have been filled with despair up until now), I simply must record some of what transpired, and some of what I'm feeling.

First of all, and most important, right this minute, I am not overwhelmed with sadness and hopelessness. This in itself astounds me. I also do not feel alone. I am somehow, right this minute, convinced you are here with me. I feel momentarily overcome when I think that I cannot touch you, or hug you, or laugh with you, or cry with you. But I am comforted to know that you are with me so often.

Yesterday, all day, I felt this delicious anticipation, as if I had a date. I felt like I was going to see you, and I had the distinct feeling that you were doing the same thing over there, even though there is no time where you are. I felt as if you were pacing around waiting for me to finally get to James so we could be together again. Meeting James was wonderful. He's instantly likable and has an innocence about him that makes him easy to trust.

As time goes on, and I continue to digest all the evidence that was given me, I'm sure I will have many more questions for you. But what I really wanted tonight was evidence—a statement from you that you were okay. I felt that nothing less would do. Even though I had no idea what to expect, you convinced me that your beautiful spirit lives on.

So, my darling, welcome back in whatever form you exist. I'll take whatever I can get until we are together again. Tell Poppa I remember Niagara Falls. I'm so glad you are with Nana. Sunday is Father's Day. Daddy should be much comforted by your messages of love. I know I am.

I don't anticipate any future joy in my life. I will still find myself in the depths of despair most of the time. But tonight I feel a strange reassurance that you and I are not over. And for that I thank you, and I thank James Van Praagh.

I love you, Peter, and I miss you. I shall try to go on to my natural end with some dignity and grace. But I shall spend every day of my life looking forward to the next time we can be together. I can hardly wait.

Love always,
Mom

UPDATE

Marie has had a difficult time grieving the loss of her son, Peter. There were times when she thought she wouldn't make it. And while she continues to have her up and down days, she is able to weather her feelings as best she can. I spoke with her recently, and she told me that she keeps quite active between her full-time job and devoting herself to the Manhattan chapter of The Compassionate Friends. She has been helping other parents through their mourning process. She has also taken the time to express herself and her grief through writing, and is the editor of the Manhattan Compassionate Friends' newsletter. Marie plans to write a book about grief support, sharing her story as well as the stories of other parents whose lives have been forever changed by the death of a child. When not working, Marie tends her garden on Long Island. "There is something so spiritual about working in a garden," she told me. "As I watch my plants flower and bloom, I think of my son Peter growing up in heaven. This is a place where we can commune together. He always seems to come to me during those quiet moments in the garden."

ACCIDENTS AND DISASTERS

I am often questioned about loved ones who are killed in accidents and disasters. The first thing I am asked is, "Do they feel pain?" The answer is always, "No." At the time of the accident, or plane crash or earthquake, the spiritual self is quickly released from the physical body. A person may have felt fear and panic before death, but there is no physical pain at the time of death. The difficulty in deaths of this nature is the task of grieving by the survivors.

Accidents and disasters seem to be common occurrences nowadays. Maybe it is because we see so many of these events on the TV every evening. Because death of this kind is sudden, unexpected and, in human terms, premature, the traumatic effects on the survivors is particularly tragic. No one is prepared for the news of a loved one who died in a car accident or plane crash. It seems so unreal. You wonder if someone has made a terrible mistake and has confused you for some other poor soul who lost someone in the accident.

As you have read from the above testimony of parents whose children died in accidents, there is no easy way to deal with this sudden and tragic loss of life. The shock is so severe that most survivors are completely thrown into an altered state. They wonder why such a thing could happen, and why it was their particular loved one. These questions usually pass through their minds for quite some time. After their shock and numbness, there is usually a lot of guilt felt by surviving family members. *Why didn't I tell him to call me if he was staying out late? Why didn't I tell her to stay and change her plane reservations for the next day? Why didn't I drive him home instead of letting him take the train?*

If you were present at the time of the accident, you will feel guilty for surviving altogether. *Why was it my daughter and not me?* These types of thoughts can torment a person and drive her into some sort of serious illness. Also, members of the family may point a finger at the survivor.

When a child is lost suddenly, there is a lot of stress on a marriage. It is not uncommon for a husband and wife to separate or divorce after such a tragedy. Somehow, they blame each other, and blame themselves. They cannot come to terms with the loss. They cannot even speak about it to each other. They feel that they are the cause, and they cannot bear to even look at one another for fear of being reminded of their child's death. The memories are just too overwhelmingly painful.

Siblings also feel estranged from the family. They wonder if they should have died instead of the *favorite* brother or sister. Parents are so immersed in grief that they pay little attention to those who are living. Fear also permeates a sibling's day-today life. *What if they want to get rid of me? Maybe I remind them of _____. Maybe I can't live up to their expectations.* They feel exposed and vulnerable. That is why I stress that all the family members talk about their feelings and let them out.

From a spiritual standpoint, there really are no accidents. As you can see from the readings in this chapter, the spirit always had something to learn, and each one chose this particular death to complete a certain lesson or chapter in his soul development. As difficult as this may be to understand with our human minds, nevertheless, it is true. No one *dies* by accident. It is tragic and devastating, but a necessary experience for the one who died, as well as the survivors. All have come to learn something from this experience, and only each individual can know what that is.

 HEALING GUIDELINES

- Allow yourself to go through the complete grieving process.
- Acknowledge your anger, fear, and anxiety. It is all part of the grieving.
- Try not to blame yourself for your child's death. Guilt and blame will not bring your child back and only make your pain worse. Know that you cannot control all the events in life. There is a higher force at play.
- Communicate your hurt and pain with your spouse and other family members or friends. The longer you isolate yourself, the longer you feel empty. Force yourself to seek a therapist, if necessary, or a support group of parents who have gone through a similar situation.
- Help other children in the family to express their feel-

ings. Talk to them in the evening or a time when they
will be open to expressing themselves. Maybe they would
like to write a poem or do a drawing as a memorial to
their brother or sister.

- Be tolerant of your friends and relatives. They are grieving, too, and may not be sure how to behave in this situation. They will probably look to you to understand how
  to react and cope.
- Perhaps you can write a prayer or a poem, or pick out the
  music for the funeral or memorial service. This is a wonderful way to express your undying love for your child.
- Keep healthy. Make sure you eat adequately. Exercise by
  taking walks. If you have trouble sleeping, listen to a
  meditation tape or some relaxing music. A calming
  herbal tea can aid in relaxation, too.
- Communicate with your deceased child through
  thoughts, dreams, words, or pictures. Remember, your
  child hears your thoughts and feels all your love and pain
  in the spirit world.
- Begin a journal of your feelings and remembrances of
  your child. The strength of your memories will comfort
  you as the years go by.
- When holidays and birthdays come around, do something to celebrate them. Express your feelings. Try not to
  wallow in what could have been. Instead, try to see your
  child growing and learning in the spirit world.
- Do not begin to compare your other children to the deceased child. Each child is unique and special.
- Do not rush to remove your child's belongings or to
  change his or her room. There will be plenty of time to do
  this later when you are feeling more in control.
- Begin to explore the spiritual side of life. Open your
  thinking to the big picture of life. Prayers of an uplifting

nature are always helpful for both you and your deceased child. Perhaps you can learn new ideas that are positive in nature about life and the Universal Mind.

- If someone else was responsible for the death of your child, please find forgiveness in your heart. What you give out will come back to you. One never knows the karmic balance that was part of the situation. Try not to judge others harshly. Remember that love always begets more love.

- Celebrate the child's life. Perhaps you are drawn to participate in a cause or charity that helps children. Perhaps you have the means to form a scholarship fund to help other children. Your contribution in society is a legacy to your child.

- Try something new in your life that you have always wanted to do.

- Acknowledge how strong and powerful you really are, and channel that strength in bringing back some normalcy to your life.

- Rest assured that you will get through this experience.

- Realize that you will be united with your child when it is your time to go home to heaven. Love is the bridge while you are on earth.

Dearest Mommy

When you wonder the meaning of life and love
Know that I am with you,
Close your eyes and feel me kissing you
in the gentle breeze across your cheek.

When you begin to doubt that you shall ever see me again
Quiet your mind and hear me,
I am in the whisper of the heavens
Speaking of your love.

When you lose your identity
When you question who you are and where you are going,
Open your heart and see me.
I am the twinkle in the stars smiling down upon you,
Lighting the path for your journey.

When you awaken each morning
Not remembering your dreams
But feeling content and serene
Know that I was with you—
Filling your night with thoughts of me

When you linger in the remnant pain
Wholeness seeming so unfamiliar
Think of me and
Know that I am with you,
Touching you through the shared tears of a gentle friend
Easing the pain

As the sunrise illuminates the desert sky
In the breathtaking glory, awaken your spirit
Think of our time, all too brief, but ever brilliant.
When you were certain of us, together
When you were certain of your destiny

Know that God created that moment in time,
Just for us
Dearest Mommy, I am with you always.

—*Joanne Cacciatore*

PART III

Losses of a Different Kind

DIVORCE:
THE DEATH OF A
MARRIAGE

*H*ow many of us have experienced the heartbreak of a faded love? When a love dies, one feels flung into a world that seems precarious and empty. We feel at a loss, and we go through grief, but we may not recognize the signs. Divorce carries with it all sorts of negative connotations. No one likes the word, and no one really wants to go through it. Unfortunately, divorce is a fact of life, and like death, the end of a marriage causes mental and emotional grief. The dream of a future together has come undone. The house is empty. We no longer feel complete. Just like losing a spouse to death, we go through much of the same emotional pain because an intimate life shared together is over. Suddenly a life that once seemed so secure has come to an end, and you must figure out how to cope with this devastating change. Couples with children feel the added loss of no longer sharing in the hopes and dreams of their child's future. On top of it all, you must also face your outer family circle, friends, and acquaintances and deal with their reactions. Blame is usually the first response to a divorce, and various family members and friends usually take up sides with one spouse or the other, which only makes matters worse. So not only have you lost your spouse and feel alone, but soon afterward relatives turn a cold shoulder, and married friends no longer include you in their circle of activities. Your hurt is compounded. The isolation seems monumental.

Unfortunately, like all losses, divorce never happens at an opportune time. Often a divorce occurs just when we buy a new house or new car, or start a new job, or even have a baby. It's not unusual that major changes in our lives trigger questions in our mind about other areas of our lives as well. *Am I fulfilled? Is this what I want? Am I happy with the way my life is going?* When a couple meets individual goals, and they feel that they are headed in the same direction, then all is going well. However, when they feel they have outgrown each other, or have opposite goals or directions, divorce seems to be the only viable choice.

A divorce is usually the end result of years of unhappiness and dissatisfaction in a relationship. Often one mate feels that he hasn't grown emotionally with the other. One of the partners may have pursued different interests and goals, or her dreams and desires have changed, and she feels they will not be realized in her present situation. One or both could lose sexual interest in the other, or they realize they were never suited for one another in the first place. The dissatisfaction may also result from the various stresses of our society through jobs, children, and aging.

DIVORCE GRIEF

It is natural that people going through a divorce experience withdrawal, hurt, sadness, anger, and despair. These same feelings occur when a loved one dies. It is also typical for a husband or wife to feel betrayed. *How could she? Why did he do that to me?* They usually experience some kind of guilt. *If only I told her more often that I loved her. If only I spent more time with him. If only I didn't let him down.* These are very common reactions. So many individuals identify divorce as a failure because they believe they could have done better. They will blame themselves, and create all different types of scenarios. *I should have known this would happen. How could I have been so stupid?*

Divorce usually occurs because one partner has made the decision to end the relationship. In his or her mind, it's over. Of course, couples should seek counseling before they make a final decision. After all, we learned about relationships from our parents, and if their relationship was filled with difficulties, our experience of a good and loving relationship is limited. If we had little emotional support as children, we may not know how to emotionally support someone else. If we were abused physically or emotionally, we carry that pain inside us and transfer it to another person. But we can undo what we were taught, and it is always wise to seek help before we take the ultimate step toward divorce.

Yet when one partner decides to end the relationship, it usually comes after much contemplation. If one partner feels unfulfilled, it is likely that he becomes very rigid and has un-compromising expectations for the other partner. In situations where one partner has outgrown the relationship, she tends to internalize feelings and not express them verbally. At this point all communication breaks down to such a degree that anger and blame are the only emotions left. Reconciliation, even with the best of therapists, is highly unlikely.

If you are the one being left behind, you will more than likely feel hurt. You will probably think you have done some-thing wrong: *I'm not good enough*. The partner left behind usu-ally experiences issues of low self-esteem. In some cases the individual tends to hold on to the relationship, denying that it has come to an end. Unfortunately, this only prolongs the suf-fering, as denial bottles up deep-seated feelings of anger and shame.

KARMIC TIES

On the physical plane, divorce feels like a death. We are completely disoriented. We are hurt, outraged, and humili-ated. Most of us perceive divorce from this level and observe little else. However, on a spiritual level, there is much more going on. I have spoken to many people years after a divorce, and they all seem to say the same thing: *It was one of the key growing experiences of my life*.

From a spiritual point of view, divorce occurs because karmic obligations between two souls must be met. Souls reincarnate together during a lifetime to fulfill a soul contract. Often when we first meet a soul mate, we feel that we have met this person before. On an intuitive level, we are drawn to this individual. The results are varied. There are spiritual marriages, like Margie

and Buddy's from a previous chapter, in which two spirits per-
petuate unconditional love for each other as well as love of
self. The opposite is also true. Some relationships are doomed
from the start. We know that they are not good for us, but we
feel pulled toward the person for some inexplicable reason.
This usually means a karmic relationship has to be resolved
and the soul lesson cannot be completed without a commitment. Perhaps souls choose to work out, or burn out, their
past-life desires to create a union. This *burning out* of karma
between the two may not be resolved in one lifetime. Perhaps
we must learn independence and self-love, or we have to overcome differences and become self-reliant and trusting. Often
one soul has to repay an obligation from a previous lifetime, as
you will learn from my personal account. This is the nature of
a soul contract. It does not always mean that we are going to
live happily ever after.

Spiritual evolution is part of every soul's destiny on earth,
and each soul grows and evolves at a different rate. Most marriages fall apart because of our own unconscious behavior. It is
important to keep this in mind when trying to understand the
nature of divorce. If we can step away and look at the situation
from a larger, more universal perspective, we will understand
that we have *chosen* our particular partner to progress spiritually. If we continue to harbor ill will even after a divorce, then
we will return in another life to repeat the experience until we
learn to love.

IT WAS MEANT TO BE

I went through my own distressing and agonizing experience of divorce. Like a death, I don't think we ever completely

get over it, but hopefully we learn to reconstruct our lives in positive and fulfilling ways.

I met Karen in college. I will never forget that night. I entered college at mid-term, and I needed to get credits immediately, so I joined a college production of *Side by Side by Sondheim* as an assistant stage manager. My job involved giving cues to various stage technicians to move scenery. I also had to shine a flashlight on the exit stairs for the actors leaving the stage.

At my first rehearsal, I was watching the stage for my first cue to shine the light on the steps for the actress to exit. I was anxiously holding my flashlight when I saw a petite blonde with blue eyes and plumpish cheeks enter. The moment I saw her step onto the stage, I felt goose bumps travel up my body. I couldn't stop staring at her. When she opened her mouth to sing, it was as if a choir of heavenly angels had descended upon this earthly cherub. I could hardly contain myself. I had never seen a woman so beautiful and with such an innocence and openness about her. I felt a sense of connection with her that was unlike anything I ever felt before. I remember that I thought to myself right then and there, *I'm going to marry her one day.* This was way before I understood anything about psychic phenomena, past lives, or karma. It was just this sense of knowing I had about Karen.

As the rehearsals continued each day, I got to know Karen. At first she didn't seem to take an interest in me, but by the time the show rolled around, we were laughing each time she came off stage as I escorted her every step with my flashlight. She was quite relieved that I was there to help because she suffered from double vision due to a car accident.

Karen and I became friends very quickly, and soon we saw each other on a constant basis, sharing lunches and dinners as we discussed our backgrounds, our majors, and our plans for the future. A few months passed, and Karen and I began dating. We enjoyed each other's company very much. We went to shows and dances, had picnics in the park, and read and studied together. It was my very first serious relationship, and I was in bliss.

The relationship lasted our first year in college and through the summer. I lived about forty miles away from Karen, so during the summer I would visit her in upstate New York. Her parents, like most folks, were a little overprotective of their daughter. They tended to shield her from me, even though I was always doing my best to be considerate and charming on these visits. I felt that if Karen's parents got to know me better, they would trust me, and be happy for our relationship. However, they never showed any signs of approval.

After that summer Karen didn't return to school. It seemed her car accident had a more serious effect on her than first thought. Her back gave her a lot of trouble, and the doctors decided that she needed as much rest as possible. Our relationship began to fade, as the distance between us grew both literally and figuratively. Eventually we went our separate ways, and I was heartbroken. I couldn't believe it was over. After all, I thought I was definitely going to marry this girl. Somehow I felt cheated.

Fast-forward twelve years. I had moved from New York to California. I had just started a full-time job at Paramount Studios working as a contract coordinator. Besides shuffling the papers in the contract department, I found myself in a whole new world. I had begun to develop my psychic ability.

It had been about two and a half years since Brian Hurst first told me I was a medium. At the time I was involved in meditation circles and reading for people every night after work. I already had a waiting list three months long based on word of mouth, so I thought there had to be something to this.

I looked forward to my evenings and always felt lucky that I could communicate with spirit. I spent every night bridging the gap between the human world and the sprit world. I found the more I gazed into the incredible spirit world, the more I became filled with spirits' loving thoughts of kindness and gentleness, and the more I wanted to spread the message and let everyone in on it. I felt that if I could share it with others, our world on earth would become magical. When I saw the complete change on a person's face after communicating with a deceased child or loving family member, and felt the lightness and loving energy in the room, I knew I had found my life's work.

During the course of this great realization, I began to wonder about my relationship with Karen so many years before. Ever since I had said good-bye to her, I had never stopped thinking of her. I felt obsessed by her memory, and these haunting thoughts of her became more frequent. It seemed the more I became aware on a psychic level, the more I would think of Karen. It felt very odd. I felt as if we hadn't completed something together. These thoughts became stronger, and I found myself constantly wondering, *How is Karen? What is she doing now?*

The pressure of Karen's memory became too much, and I decided to do something about it. I called New York telephone information to check for the number under her name. Unfortunately, there was no listing with that family name at least in seventy-five percent of New York state. I was frustrated, but felt as though I had to get in contact with her. So I looked up to heaven and said out loud, *Dear friends, if I am meant to meet Karen again, to learn something from her, or to accomplish something, please have her call me.*

I still feel chills up my spine thinking about it. I thought my plea a bit bizarre, but I felt as though I had come to the end of my rope, and if it was meant to be, it would happen. The eerie response to my plea came two weeks later on a Tuesday morning at six. The phone rang, and I ran down the stairs to the kitchen. My mind was filled with horrible thoughts about someone having been hurt or having died. Needless to say, I'm not immune to having the same thoughts as anyone else. Anyway, I answered the phone, hesitant to learn of the tragedy that was ready to unfold on the other end. However, after a few pregnant pauses I heard the sound of a sweet angelic voice that I had not heard in twelve years.

"Hello, James. James Van Praagh, this is Karen . . . We went to school together. Remember me?"

Remember her? If only she knew what I had gone through! I almost fell on the floor in a faint. I kept asking myself, *Is this for real? Am I dreaming? Is this a joke?* To say the least, I was in shock. The magical and mystical world of spirit had heard my plea for help and answered it with a resounding *yes.*

"Hello, James. Is that you? Can you hear me?"

"Yes, Karen. How are you? I can hardly believe I am talking to you." I was in a daze and sweating profusely.

"It's funny, I have been thinking about you for a long time, and even more so in the past two weeks. I met someone last week who knew your brother, so I called him and got your phone number in California. I hope you don't mind that I called."

I was trying to remain as calm as possible. I spat out, "Oh, yes, it's great you called. Funny, I was thinking about you, too. How have you been? What have you been doing? Where do you live?"

I couldn't stop. I wanted to catch up on the past twelve years. I soon asked one question too many because along with my giddiness came a sense of trepidation. I didn't want to hear the answer that was about to come next.

"Oh, I am fine. I'm married now."

I heard it! Oh, no. The word I didn't want to hear. My heart sank.

"Married?" I said, somewhat aloof.

"Married!" I repeated in a high C, saying it over and over again, thinking that somehow it would change the situation and return us to our single days at college.

"Yes. I've been married a couple of years. My husband works in the media. How are you? What are you up to these days? You know, I have thought about you through the years."

I felt a glimmer of hope when she admitted that she had been thinking of me, too.

"Oh, I'm not doing much. I moved to Los Angeles to become a sitcom writer. Right now I am working at Paramount in their contract department."

I didn't want to mention anything about my psychic work. I didn't want to scare her off just when we were getting reacquainted. At the least, I thought we could be friends. I didn't want her to think I had turned into a psycho by mentioning I was a psychic.

Karen and I chatted for a good half hour, catching up on life. She explained that how she had become a prominent individual in the born again Christian movement. I was all the more happier that I hadn't shared everything with her.

She said, "I was reminiscing about the good old days and thought of you."

We spent the remaining time laughing and joking, and recalling old friends and events that made us feel good. Our time on the phone felt comfortable, and it reassured me that we still shared a mutual understanding after all these years. We exchanged phone numbers with the promise of speaking again in the near future.

During the next two weeks Karen and I spent many hours

on the phone. I was a little confused because I knew she was married and nothing could ever come of our friendship. But I was so happy that I didn't want to burst the bubble just yet. I rationalized my fears as "just good old fun."

However, that fun took a more serious turn when Karen decided to visit me in California. *Was this possible?* I could not believe it, and thought the spirit world was playing a major joke on me. Two weeks later, with suitcase in tow, Karen stepped off the plane, and time stood still.

The moment we saw each other, *boom*, something happened! No one had to be psychic to feel that. There was an electricity between us; it was almost embarrassing to look at one another. Yet we both knew it was real and that our reunion could end up being very dangerous.

That night we went out for dinner at the local Sizzler restaurant. As I stared at her, I noticed that she had barely aged. She had kept her keen sense of humor and grace. At the same time, I had this agonizing feeling that something was not perfect with this picture. Something somewhere seemed a little off. Karen went on about her life in the church and admitted how unfulfilled she felt with that type of calling. It was then that I let the cat out of the bag. I had to be honest with her.

"I'm a psychic," I gulped, squinting my eyes in readiness for a reprimand and a ticket straight to hell.

Surprisingly, she looked at me wide eyed and replied, "You, too? Oh, thank God. I thought I was the only one!"

What a relief! We both went into details about our psychic experiences and attributes.

"We don't refer to it as spirit in my church," she explained.

The evening turned out to be enlightening and weird at the same time. It seemed that we were two kindred souls reunited, and my only thought was, *What do we do now?*

Karen and I spent the next week discussing everything. She admitted that she was on a temporary leave from her husband. She confessed, "I don't feel connected to him anymore." She said that she needed someone who was more caring and supportive and interested in the same things. I think this is where I came into the picture. It was obvious that we still loved each other, and we sincerely wanted to spend time together. I remember looking up to heaven and hearing the words of spirit: *Be careful what you wish for!*

Karen never made it back East. She felt free and alive again. She did not want to go back to the church. I had to make sure that her decision to stay was based on her change in attitude and not because of me. I didn't want any karmic repercussions. At the same time, I wasn't so sure that I wanted to get involved with Karen, or make a commitment to her, although there was still the feeling that I was supposed to be with her. Karen filed for divorce and began living with me. We lived together for several months, and each day seemed better than the next. Different things would happen, strange coincidences that led me to believe we were meant to be with each other.

A friend of mine helped Karen get a job at a Fortune 500 company, and she quickly adapted to a new lifestyle. Like any couple, we began to learn more and more about each other. Spirit was a main focus in our relationship, and Karen began to sit in my meditation circles. I really enjoyed being with her, but something was a little out of sync, and I couldn't quite figure it out. On many occasions, when I would leave for a period of time, Karen would become anxious enough to contemplate suicide. She would often say things like, "Please, don't go. I feel scared. I can't trust myself. I might hurt myself."

Eventually this anxiety developed into recurring nightmares about leaving the church and feeling abandoned. We found a wonderful therapist who worked with both of us. She spent a great deal of time working with Karen's abandonment issues. The therapy was by all means a success, and Karen seemed quite healthy. The nightmares began to subside.

Our relationship grew day by day, and our closeness became stronger. It seemed a natural progression to marry. Something inside kept urging me to marry Karen, as if it was in the cards. You'd think that being psychic, I would have known for sure. However, like any other human, I have my own lessons to learn. It's difficult to read myself, as my emotions color my judgment about myself.

When I asked Karen to marry me, she felt some trepidation. I interpreted her feelings as her misgivings about being married again. On the other hand, I felt for some reason it was meant to be. I invited the spirit world to assist us in the decision and asked, *Friends, if the marriage is meant to be, please give us signs.*

We kept ourselves open so we would be aware of these signs if and when they occurred. Several months passed, and we decided to look for wedding bands, but we had trouble finding what we wanted. After looking at what seemed to be thousands of rings, we walked into a store in Santa Monica, California. A very friendly man with a strong Italian accent by the name of Leo greeted us. We told him what we wanted. He smiled, ushered us over to a glass case, and showed us a pair of wedding rings. Karen and I exchanged looks. The rings were the exact design we had discussed. We couldn't believe it. We asked the jeweler to size them, so we could pick them up at the end of the following week.

The next week we were at a friend's house for a barbecue and mentioned that we had found the perfect wedding rings but still needed to find an engagement ring to match. She suggested we call her friend who owned a jewelry store and wrote his name and number for us. The next day when I called the jewelry store, the number seemed familiar. A man with a strong accent answered, "Expertise Jewelry." Again, the name sounded familiar. I explained what I was looking for, and he suggested that we come to his shop in Santa Monica. I was dumbfounded. No wonder it sounded familiar. It was the exact same place we had been a week before. I asked him if he knew Leo, and he told me that Leo was his father. I thought this had to be a sign from spirit.

The following Sunday afternoon Karen and I went strolling through a mall. I said, "Why don't we look for your wedding dress today?"

She turned to me and said, "I don't think we could find what I'm looking for in a department store."

Yet Karen went along to appease me. "I still don't think I will find what I want."

"What do you want?" I asked.

"A Jessica McClintock gown with ivory lace. I saw it in a magazine."

With that in mind, we went through Macy's double doors and rode the escalator to Formal Dresses.

As we got off the escalator, the first mannequin we spotted was decked out in a gorgeous ivory-colored lace dress.

Karen stopped. "That's it!"

I glowed. "See!"

"It's gorgeous, but I'm sure it's not the right size."

We fumbled for the tag. The label read Jessica McClintock, size twelve! We stared at each other with our mouths open. Was this another sign from spirit? We located a salesperson and asked her to check the price.

"This is the last dress, and it went on sale today." I think this convinced me that everything was falling into place and that our marriage was meant to be.

The wedding was held at a friend's beautiful ocean-view

house in Malibu. It was a simple ceremony that we wrote ourselves. Perhaps one of the most profound signs was yet to occur. As we recited our vows, two doves circled around the area
until the ceremony ended. It was truly a beautiful and heartfelt
experience, and one I will always remember.

Karen and I went on a brief honeymoon, and quickly got
back to everyday activities. Soon after, I had this overwhelming feeling that I had accomplished something. I don't know
how to explain it, except that I felt something was completed.

We bought a house and enjoyed decorating it, filling it with
new and attractive furnishings. We adopted two dogs along
with several stray cats. But no amount of furniture or animals
could fill what seemed to be missing. After we settled into our
house, our relationship slowly began to take a downward turn.
Like many other couples, each person learns and grows at different rates, and this, I believe, happened to us. I think that
our goals were leading us in diverse directions, and as each day
passed, we grew more apart. We were in counseling for
months, and after attempting a myriad of partnering exercises,
I came to the conclusion that the marriage was over. It lasted
a year and a half. On one hand, I had the feeling that something had been accomplished, though I wasn't sure what it
was, and on the other, I felt very sad.

Learning a Lesson

No matter who initiates a divorce, it always takes two to
make a marriage and two to end it. As our marriage disinte-
grated, Karen and I both experienced anger, guilt, and blame.
It was one of the most emotionally challenging times in my
life. At times I thought, *I don't even know this person.* On some
level, it didn't make sense to me. I felt I had given my all to
make our marriage work, and it still wasn't working out. I be-

gan to question, *Is this what we were supposed to go through spiritually? What about the signs from spirit?* This was especially confusing to me because I thought we had spirit's blessing. Yet here we were, breaking up.

In order to learn from this experience, I had to take responsibility for my decisions. I started to question my motives and intentions for getting a divorce.

Why am I frustrated with the marriage?

Do I feel sad, lonely, and depressed?

Do I feel Karen and I are not connecting with each other anymore?

Do we have the same goals?

Do we respect each other's differences?

Do we have control issues?

Am I happy?

Is my soul being nourished?

This last question was the most important of all, and regrettably, my response was *no*. If a marriage becomes emotionally, physically, mentally, or spiritually deprived, one cannot stay in that situation. I came to the realization that we were two souls who had to learn something from each other. I had to see our relationship as an opportunity to grow, even though at the time it did not make sense. Beyond the pain and suffering, I had to find the love and joy. I had to find happiness within myself.

Several months later, I went to see a healer and clairvoyant by the name of Michael Tamura, who was strongly recommended by a friend. Michael is a man with an incredible amount of wisdom and accuracy. The first time I met him, I knew he had a great gift of insight.

At our first meeting Michael assured me that he had never seen or heard of me. I was relieved. I felt it would be a more accurate reading if he had no idea who I was. Michael began the reading by staring above my head and moving his fingers and hands in an upward and downward motion.

He then asked, "You have been married, yes?"

"Yes," I replied.

"This girl is short with blonde curls, correct?"

"Yes, that is right." It was obvious to me that he was on the right track.

"Yes, I see her energy around you. She is still holding on to you in some ways. You and she have just cleaned a karmic debt. I see that you have severed the marriage ties, and I understand why."

At last, I thought to myself. Somebody was finally going to resolve this confusion and tell me what my marriage was all about. I was grateful for any clarification.

"Please continue. I would like some insight on this matter."

Michael explained, "You see, in another life you and Karen were gypsies. You traveled together in wagons and lived in one village or another. In that lifetime, which seems to be the last one you experienced with her, she begged you to marry her and you promised you would. Several days before the marriage celebration, you got cold feet and left. She was so despondent and filled with such self-hatred that she decided to end her life. She drank poison and killed herself. This set up a karmic debt between the two of you. In between lives you promised to resolve the karmic repercussions of that situation. Do you understand?"

"Perfectly," I replied.

Michael continued, "You had to overcome the fear of commitment, and at the same time help her to believe in the strength of herself."

Michael's every word struck a chord deep down in my soul. I felt as though I were looking into a mirror and seeing my life clearly. I finally understood why I'd had this unrelenting sense of needing to be with Karen after our courtship in college. Michael's perceptiveness also shed light on Karen's feelings of abandonment, isolation, and suicide. She had to experience these same feelings over again in order to have an opportunity to grow beyond them. She had to learn to have faith in herself, and I had to help her. It certainly put everything in perspective. Spirit moved us to connect in this life to fulfill our karmic obligation and learn from it. I was relieved that I had accomplished what I had promised to do. At that point I had no more doubt about my decision to divorce. I felt we had completed what we needed to do and were free to move on.

In hindsight, my marriage and divorce from Karen sounds simple enough, but learning the lesson was not so easy. As humans, our thoughts and emotions stand in our way. We've all heard the expression: *You have to get out of your own way.* That's exactly what we have to do. We have to let go of "I'm right, you're wrong" attitudes. Grieving our loss is only normal and is necessary to get through divorce. So many of us don't understand that all the feelings that come out of a divorce are the stages of grief. Once we realize that, we may be able to let life flow rather than trying to hold on to the past.

Life after Divorce

On a psychological level, being single again can stir many anxieties and insecurities within us. The most obvious is the fear of losing financial stability. Suddenly you are a one-income household, and you can no longer spend money extravagantly. If you have children to support, it becomes all the more fearful. In many cases a divorced person must find additional sources of income, which in turn leaves him or her even more resentful and emotionally drained. Then there are household responsibilities that you have to do alone. You go through the stages of grief just as if someone died. You feel isolated. You retreat into denial. You think, *This can't be happening to me.* Denying your feelings is a common phenomenon. If we can't feel it, it must not exist. I believe our denied feelings are the cause of most of society's problems. Acts of violence and abuse stem from negative feelings that have been deeply repressed and denied.

When you experience feelings of isolation, loneliness, and numbness, I suggest you seek help from friends or support groups. This is the time to get it off your chest. Holding on to your feelings of hurt, anger, and self-loathing only makes you feel inadequate and miserable. Instead of letting these feelings propagate, seek ways to fill the void inside you. If you can begin to acknowledge the loss of a relationship, you will have taken the first step on the road to recovery. You must realize that there are many adjustments to make along the way. By reaching out, you are moving toward closing the wounds and healing yourself. When you can speak to someone you trust and respect, and express those internal feelings, you will feel some sort of relief. This type of purging is always good for the soul. Second, when you discuss your feelings with another, you will get a fresh perspective on the situation. Someone else's feedback may help you to see a problem differently and clear up some of the confusion you may be feeling and possibly create some degree of closure.

CHILDREN AND GRIEF

Between lives, Karen and I had agreed to clear our karma, and once that was achieved, there was no further need to be together. Every situation is unique, however. For many couples their karma includes having children. Remember that each member of a family chooses the conditions under which he or she enters the world, including the children of parents who divorce. Nevertheless, the feelings, concerns, emotional and psychological states of children whose parents divorce must be taken into consideration during the process, and so often they are not.

By the time a couple divorces, most children have already witnessed months, perhaps years, of conflict. Because they are much more sensitive than adults, children take in every thought, nuance, emotion, and seen and unseen action. Everything is recorded in their subconscious minds. As early as the age of three, a child registers the emotional scars of a divorce. So don't think young children are impervious to what is happening. Thoughts and feelings are buried deep within a child's psyche and may not be obvious to the adults around them.

Older children usually go into some sort of a tailspin, and wonder what is going to happen to them when their parents break up. No matter the quarrels, abuse, and upheaval, a child still wants to hold on to the security of having a mother and father. Children will not verbalize how they feel, but they will feel displaced. *Where do I go? Who will take care of me?* The same is true of a child whose parent dies. Children feel the loss, but do not know how to verbalize their feelings. Everything is internalized and magnified. Children usually feel *wrong* or *at fault* in some way, and these feelings can shape the rest of their lives. Sometimes these unexpressed emotions manifest in behaviorally destructive ways.

Children of divorce feel caught in the middle of something over which they have no control. They love their parents, yet feel they must choose one over the other. How difficult do you think it is for a child to make this decision? It's too hard.

Sometimes parents deliberately put their children in the middle of a divorce, which only creates more fear inside a child. Many parents compromise about custody, and a child lives with one and is visited by the other.

There are many similarities between losing a parent through death and losing a parent through divorce. First of all, a child usually feels to blame: *Did I do something wrong? Am I being punished for misbehaving?* A child has a lot of confusion. He may not know how to act around others. A child may feel embarrassed especially among peers. Children may feel like crying, but don't want to show their emotions because they don't want to hurt one or both parents. A child can become angry or moody: *I have been abandoned. I am powerless in this situation. They don't care about me.*

If a child is raised in a religious household, she may question God about the situation. *Is God punishing me?* Physically, children may suffer from insomnia, loss of appetite, and a slowdown in activity.

Every child has to cope with adult behavior as he grows up, and that is difficult enough under the best of circumstances. When a divorce takes place, a child has to cope under the worst of circumstances. Depending on the custody agreement, a mother may feel that she has lost control of her child's life, and she may become intrusive and domineering. She may tell the father what he may or may not do for his child. This behavior creates a wall between the two of them, and a father becomes resentful. He gets back at her by withholding information. This is a very difficult situation for children. The mother only wants what's best for her child, yet her controlling behavior, which is a manifestation of her anger and resentment, is causing more trouble. The father wants to establish his own unique relationship with his child, to show his worth as a parent, yet at the same time he may do things just to hurt his ex-wife. This only creates misunderstanding and mistrust for a child, who usually suffers in silence. Often parents are so caught up in their own feelings that they cannot help their children go through their own grief process. Parents may even discard their children's feelings because they themselves are unable to cope. The parent must take the lead in the situation and become attentive to a child's moods and behavior. It is up to parents to help their children express themselves.

Another problem occurs when a parent brings home a new mate. A child may feel threatened by the new stranger. *Doesn't she love me anymore? I'm not enough. Maybe I'm in the way, and I'll have to leave.* To add to a child's fear of losing his parent to someone else, or feeling cast aside, the other parent may criticize or condemn the new mate. This only adds confusion to uncertainty. In this situation, the most important question a parent must ask is: What is best for my child's psychological and emotional well-being? Parents need to put themselves in their children's place and be brutally honest. They must realize that their children absorb their negative behavior not only emotionally and psychologically, but also psychically. Children don't understand why they feel bad or down. They are like sponges, soaking up their parent's desolation.

I have done readings for a few children during my professional career. Children are not ready to fully understand or express feelings, thoughts, and psychic sensibilities. I did read for one boy whose coach died. The spirit assured the boy that he was safe and all right in heaven. The child was very relieved. I think most children want to know that about the adults who leave them. They want to know that everything is all right. They want to know that nothing bad has happened to them. Ultimately, they want to know that Mommy or Daddy is safe.

Helping a Child Heal

As parents, we must be sensitive to our children's feelings during this difficult time of their lives. Talk to your children. Let them know what is happening. Express to them your heartfelt emotions, but don't blame one another. This is not about making a child a referee in a fight. Nor is it about making your child a scapegoat.

The worst thing a parent can do is try to hide a divorce from a child. The same is true about hiding a death from a child. Parents think they are shielding their child from unnecessary heartache, but this only makes a child feel left out, as if he doesn't matter. Treat your child as you would like to be treated. Let her know that she is an integral part of the family unit. Design the communication according to a child's age and level of understanding. If she is young, perhaps the situation would be better understood if depicted in drawings or pictures, or references to something within the child's world. If he is older, sit down and have an honest discussion. It is imperative that parents talk to their children and help them to verbalize their inner feelings and concerns. However, don't expect a child to react or respond like an adult. Children tend not to speak about their emotions; they tend to act them out, so parents need to be observant of behavior patterns. Is the child moody or listless? Does he stay by himself too much, or does she stay out too late? Our job as parents is to pay attention to our children, not the other way around.

The most substantial thing you can do is to show love, affection, and support. Include your children in any discussions that may help them to express their grief and loss. Continue to have a feeling of love in the home. Parents can always ask for love in the form of hugs from their child. This will help your child see that she plays an important part in your healing process, as well as reinforcing the bond that you are still very much together. A child needs to know you still love him, no matter how life changes.

It's difficult at best to identify how a child feels, or how a child grieves. Sometimes years pass before a child tells you that she felt to blame about your divorce. That is why a parent needs to discuss the matter with the child as soon as possible. A child has to know from you that he is not guilty for your separation and is not being punished for doing something wrong. You don't want these negative feelings to fester within the child and years later show up as an inferiority complex that leads to fatalistic behavior like alcoholism, drug abuse, or violence.

Once you share with your children, allow them to ask questions and offer solutions to problems. Let them feel involved. Whatever the situation or limitation with a spouse, both parents need to continue to establish an amicable relationship for the welfare of the child. Create a positive atmosphere in which your child feels safe to be inquisitive and resourceful. Parents should explain to their children that they still can love someone but not live with them. Let your child know that he or she is part of a family. Above all, keep assuring your children that they are safe and very loved.

HEALING GUIDELINES

- Allow yourself to go through the complete grieving process.
- Assess your marriage. What are you feeling? Establish and review the situation on all levels: emotional, mental, spiritual, and physical.
- Relax and meditate. Bring yourself back to a centered

and balanced position. When you are centered and properly grounded, everything is easier to deal with. You can see things from a much clearer perspective by not letting your emotions cloud your thoughts.

- Stop feeling as though you are the victim. Begin to take control of your life instead of feeling sorry for yourself.

- Bring positive energy into all areas of your life. Try as best as you can to see this as a renewal of yourself and another chance at life.

- Begin to let go. Stop trying to control the situation. Turn your anger around and use the energy of that feeling to deal with the situation in a positive manner.

- Develop and establish a supportive network of friends and social groups in order to begin life once again as a single person. This might include taking a class or entering a new career. Give yourself time to explore every option available and any pursuit in which you might have interest.

- Familiarize yourself with the effects of divorce and grieving through books, seminars, and even the Internet. There is a lot of information available. Learn what you need to know to rebuild a new life.

- Slow down and take your time. You do not have to do everything at once. Give yourself some well-deserved breathing room. Do not throw yourself into another relationship without taking the time to grieve and recover. This is never fair to a new relationship.

- Create a new family unit for your children. You need to reestablish the family and your parental roles in this new situation, excluding any form of control and manipulation. One needs to discuss financial arrangements, changing schools, and a visitation schedule. Do this as amicably as possible for the welfare of the child.

- Develop your new life by including your children in the decision process.
- Keep a journal of your feelings and the situation and what you would like for yourself in the future.
- Forgive your partner and yourself, even if you can't rationalize the divorce. Try to understand the other person's feelings. Realize that the person you once loved has changed. Let go and wish the person well. This was a lesson for both of you. Both of you will be better for it in the long run.
- Remember that you are never alone. Love is all around you; it is *not* taken away from you. You are made of love, and this earth is rich with opportunities to love again.

7

PASSAGES

*N*o one teaches us to expect failure, sickness, poverty, and growing old. On the contrary. We are geared toward making a success of our lives, to be all that we can be, to go for it, and just do it. But what happens when a crisis such as an illness or a disaster enters the picture? Most of us go into a state of shock. We don't know what to do. We are unable to cope. Any loss, even a minor one, is important. So then, how do we face crisis and loss in our lives? The answer is that we grieve.

When our lives are disrupted by a death of a loved one, we are immediately thrown into mourning and sorrow. Grieving is a natural consequence. But grief is a complex

thing, and far more encompassing than death of the body.
There are a myriad of life experiences that can also cause us to
feel at a loss. Some are necessary because they force us to
change, move on, and let go. Yet we are thrown into a grieving process because of those very reasons. There are necessary
losses, such as growing older or our children leaving home.
Other experiences of loss include chronic illness, retirement,
loss of a job or home or savings, disasters like floods and fires,
accidents, homelessness, disability, mental illness, infertility,
and caring for the elderly or sick. Still other losses are more
ambiguous, such as losing our confidence, memory, freedom,
power, dignity, or not reaching a goal, a dream, or an expectation.

Everyday life is filled with attachments to and investments
in someone or something. We get so caught up in these attachments that we think they will last forever. However, when
something is gone or taken from us, when our health fails, our
money dwindles, and our children move out, we experience
the vulnerability of loss and stages of grief. These life experiences disturb us emotionally, but we may not know that we are
grieving. Perhaps we think that we don't even have a right to
grieve. We must understand our feelings and behaviors linked
to loss and realize that as hard as it may be, it is through loss
that we develop and grow.

Life is a series of emotional tugs and pulls and is certainly
filled with stress, unhappiness, and uncertainty. We see it all
around us. Denial and withdrawal permeate so much of our
lives. We vaguely understand why we feel depressed, confused,
rejected, or angry. Our habits, early childhood conditioning,
and ego influences also sway us one way or another. There are
no simple answers to our malaise. Even my telling you to feel
better doesn't necessarily make it so. That is your choice. On a
spiritual level, we have promises to keep and lessons to master.

As life's road twists and turns, there are always moments to learn about ourselves.

When life is disrupted by loss, we can either proceed or withhold. If we push our feelings of loss and sorrow deeper inside, we truly do permit hopelessness and helplessness to seep into our being. If we connect with what we are feeling and learn from it, then we have a chance of moving beyond the pain. We have to go through the grieving process and discover for ourselves the opportunities that await us beyond our suffering.

The spirit world has instilled one profound teaching in me, and that is, we are here to accept ourselves and the world around us with love and compassion. If we could learn this one thing, we would be more content. We would feel better about ourselves and enjoy what we do have. We would understand that change is inevitable, and we would feel good enough to handle whatever comes our way. We could throw away our bottles of Prozac or alcohol or whatever it is that numbs us. We would realize that come what may, we know that the experience has purpose, and its purpose is for our spiritual growth. As I said in *Reaching to Heaven,* we come here so that our souls may evolve. That is the only journey that is worthwhile.

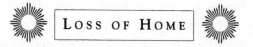

LOSS OF HOME

Losing our home to a disaster, old age, or financial loss, or because we are relocating for a new job and are forced to move, are all cause for grieving. Even when we want to move, changing our residence is a highly stressful event. It can be very confusing and frightening. We hope that we made the right choice, but we are uncertain because we don't know what to expect. If we are forced to move from our home, then the feelings of anxiety are compounded. When we move away from or lose our homes, we lose some part of our identities. In our old homes we had friends and acquaintances. When we move to someplace new, we become invisible. No one knows us, and we don't know anyone. We feel unsettled, downhearted, and even chaotic. Boxes line the rooms, and nothing is in place. We wonder what will happen to us in this new place. Everything is unfamiliar, and our human side tends to cling to what is familiar. We wonder if we will ever feel comfortable again. We wonder if our lives will return to normal.

Parents also have their children's feelings to consider. Often children have a harder time moving than adults. They are losing their friends and schoolmates. That is very difficult for a child. When I was in grammar school, one of my best friends moved away because his father lost his job and they had to move in with relatives. It was a sad day for me. He wasn't very happy, either, but he put on a good face for his family. In those days, people didn't move around a lot, so moving was a big event. We promised that we would keep in touch, and he did call me once. After that I never heard from him again. It was as if he disappeared off the face of the earth. I'm sure he had a hard time adjusting to a new school, new friends, and living with other relatives. Children tend to become quiet and reclusive as if they have been cast aside. They feel that they don't fit into the already established cliques. It's very scary, and they get "sick" a lot the first year of adjustment just to stay home. Children can't express exactly how they feel; all they know is that they don't belong. They have lost their identities because their sense of self was wrapped up in their old, familiar surroundings. Because it is so emotionally draining on children, it is important to talk with them during a move.

Moving away often means that we are going through a transition in another area of life as well, to start or change a career, for instance. When I moved from New York, it took me a while to get used to the way things were done in California. For one thing, I had to get a car, something we didn't need at home. I had to make friends because I didn't know anyone in Los Angeles. I had a lot of friends back home that knew me all through school, but I was merely a shadow in my new environment. I had to find out where to get my car serviced, and places to eat that were good, that kind of stuff. In essence, I had to build a new life. For a while I felt depressed because I missed my family and friends and everything I loved and cherished. *People know me back home; no one knows me here. Maybe this is a big mistake. Why did I move anyway?* All of these thoughts ran continually through my mind. I did want to create a new life by starting a career in TV. I had to be in a place that could offer me that chance. So with all my anxiety, all my misgivings, I was forced to decide whether to stay and reach for my dream, or go back home to where I felt comfortable. Letting go was necessary even if it was painful. After about two years I finally began to feel at home.

When I look at disasters on the news, I see so many people losing their homes and all their personal possessions. It's painful to watch, and I can only imagine how painful it is for those going through such a loss. These are times for grieving. Losing our homes, moving to another home, whether in the same area, or out of state, fills us with sadness, distress, and discouragement. It is only normal to grieve our loss. Often this is hard to do, because at the same time we are trying to put our life back to normal. If we have to relocate, we have to make new friends. This usually means putting on a happy face even though we don't feel like it. So we mask our true feelings in public and harbor our secret feelings in private. Starting over, whether in a new home, new job, new career, new way of life, can cause a sense of hopelessness. We are completely vulnerable. From the moment we realize that we are leaving behind the familiar—our loved ones, friends, perhaps certain places and events that were meaningful—we begin the process of grieving. Our emotions run the gamut from anger and disappointment to fear, sadness, and longing for what we once had.

Don't try to sugar-coat your feelings. Allow yourself to feel. You will probably experience sadness at first. When you arrive at your new home, you may feel numb or indifferent. You may get angry at yourself, your spouse, or your children. Your children may feel a lot of resentment toward you and you toward them. Consider these feelings normal, and that eventually they will subside.

Most of us want to avoid the pain of loss and grief. We are so programmed to get over it, or get on with it, or "get a life" that we push down any feelings that are contrary to society's point of view. More and more I believe these suppressed feelings emerge as violence in our world. We can't express, we don't express, or we're afraid to appear vulnerable to others. Instead we lash out in our cars as "road rage," or in our workplace, as in "going postal," or we take it out on our family in abusive ways. We need to respect our own feelings; otherwise we will not understand other people's feelings. We must go through these complex feelings if we want to get better. Grieving is actually beneficial. It helps us to let go, move on, and adapt. The more flexible we become in our thinking and being, the more we open ourselves to self-awareness and growth.

When I was a kid, moving from house to house was rare. People generally stayed put. But nowadays people move a lot. We have become a restless society, uprooting ourselves from city to city, and to different states and countries. Family members live hundreds of miles from one another. We don't stay long enough in one place to establish roots and a connection

a person feel a wasting away of physical capacities and func-
tioning, but he faces the ultimate fear—the death of the body.
One of the most common reactions is feeling a loss of control
over one's own life. With a terminal illness, one feels a loss for
any future and the role she has played in society at large. Families not only confront the loss of their loved one's vitality and
place among the family, but also the loss of their normal way of
living. There is regret and remorse for what was and what
never will be again. There is deep sadness and pain. That was
certainly the case when my mother had a stroke. Not only was
she suffering, but we had to watch her suffer, feeling helpless
and inadequate. We saw a perfectly wonderful human being
fall apart, and there was nothing we could do about it, except
make her as comfortable as possible as she withered away.

There are also the practical matters to worry about, such as
doctor visits, nursing care, and expenses related to the illness.
Family members may become resentful of their loved one's illness. Normal, everyday tasks tend to be disrupted. Watching
our loved one's health deteriorate is not only frightening but
reminds us of our own vulnerability to disease. In a moment
everything that we considered routine is uprooted. If we are
caretakers of the ill, we spend most of the day focused on illness: calls to the doctor, tests, medication, hospitalization, and
the like. Little time is left for tending to our own needs. So not
only do we feel the loss of the person whom we are helping,
but we are losing our own identities to the illness. If an illness
lasts for a considerable length of time, we may feel terribly
cheated out of years of our lives.

I had firsthand experience of caregiving when I volunteered
during the AIDS crisis in the 1980s. Like many of the volunteers, I spent many hours tending to the everyday, basic needs
of the people with this illness. I would take them to doctors'
appointments, get their medications, make sure they had

meals for the days ahead, help with their insurance paperwork, visit them in the hospital, and things like that. After a while I had come to know many people as members of my extended family. As the disease debilitated a person's body and mind, I had to stand by and watch each one suffer and pass away. I remember attending dozens of memorial services, all within a short period of time. Like casualties in war, so many people died so quickly, and it was heartbreaking. Eventually the disease took its toll on the volunteers as well, and after a few years I had to withdraw from service. Like many caregivers, I was burned out. I was in a constant state of mourning at the loss of so many friends to this disease. In a way, I felt as if I was leaving unfinished business, but as difficult as it was, I had to move on. In a way, I had to get my life back. I think all caregivers face this dilemma. You need to know when it's time to pass the torch to someone else and get through the grieving process.

If you have an illness and are facing your own death, you are in the process of very real grief. You have to come to the realization that you no longer are able to control your life in the way you once did. Often you have to leave decisions for your health in the hands of someone else. There are no words for the feelings one faces when the end is near. For many in this situation, depression is quite common. You are forced to abandon hope, dreams, and any future desires. You are labeled a sick person, and everything that you do, and that is done for you, is seen through this perspective. If you had status and power in the community or at work, you no longer are viewed in the same way. If you were responsible for income of your family, you feel shame that you have let everyone down. It's as if your identity has been yanked out of you, and a new one has replaced it—one that suggests that you are not a viable person, and instead are a drain on your loved ones. This new identity lasts until the end of your life, and is devastating to your self-worth.

People who lose an arm, a leg, their eyesight or hearing also feel inadequate and worthless to some extent. Amputation of any part of one's body is cause for deep grieving and despondency. We identify ourselves so much with our bodies that we believe we are no longer whole individuals. Many people see themselves as freaks because part of them has been cut off, and it is lost forever. Many issues of self-worth and self-esteem must be dealt with. Some people are able to conquer their self-loathing and live life with a new perspective. The many people in wheelchairs, blind, or deaf have shown us that life still can be lived to the fullest. We see it every day. Yes, there is a loss to the body, but *never* a loss to our soul, our divinity, and our true selves.

When one faces the news that she has a malignancy and has to have a mastectomy, one deals with so many mixed emotions. Due to the burden placed on women by society, women see losing a breast as a loss of their beauty, femininity, and identity as a woman. This is coupled with the anxiety that the malignancy might spread. I have met several women who have looked back at this experience in their lives as one of self-reflection and self-awareness. Recently my good friend Carol had a mastectomy, and I asked about her feelings after the operation.

"James, it really opened my eyes to a lot of things about my life. For one thing, I don't take anything for granted anymore, not a single day. I don't have time for gossip and petty people who care only about their superficial belongings." Carol confided that she attempts to find the most joy out of every situation in her life. "This was devastating to me, but also an opportunity to reevaluate who my real friends were. Most of my life, it was very hard for me to accept anything from anyone. I was usually the giver, and it was unthinkable for me to be on the receiving end of a situation. But gradually I had to come to terms with my pattern of fulfilling other people's expectations without asking for anything for myself. I always thought that was wrong of me to do. I had to learn how to receive the love people wanted to give me, or anything they wanted to give me. It was very hard to readjust my thinking. I actually had to force myself to appreciate someone's kindness and help. I realized that I didn't believe I deserved to be loved or even looked upon as a person with something to offer. I felt that if I kept doing for others, they would like me better and think I was a good person. I was only lying to myself. Most of the time I felt cheated and resentful, and not loved at all."

Carol said that after her mastectomy, she had very little time to spend in denial. I was shocked by the cavalier way in which she handled life after her surgery. Looking back, I believe she acquired a very healthy attitude. She was no longer motivated by fear. Instead she understood that she had an opportunity to change parts of her life that were false. She opened herself to the possibility of being more daring than she ever was. She told me, "It is such a great feeling to know that you are not your breasts, or any other part of your physical body. That you are a soul encased in a body, and that is the part that needs to be nurtured and fulfilled."

Fortunately for Carol, her malignancy could be treated, and today she is well and on the way to recovery. As she faced what could have been a terminal illness, she decided to get a whole new perspective on life. For those whose illness is not treatable, they, too, must come to a realization. One of the things I have learned from my spirit friends is that we are more than our bodies, and must begin to focus on the spiritual side of life, especially if we have neglected it. This is a time to make amends, tie up loose ends, and say all the things you were afraid to say. Talk to your family and friends. Let them know how you feel, but try not to blame others. Often we are so shut off from our feelings that we don't know how to express our real selves. But you can use your illness as an opportunity to pay attention to yourself and listen inwardly. In the midst of the confusion, you may be feeling alone, afraid, angry, discouraged, awkward, abandoned, and sorry for yourself. You may feel envious of those who are healthy and full of life. Family members may be feeling overwhelmed, overworked, and flustered. If you can't talk to a family member, it is important that you seek support from a group or a therapist. The same goes for the others involved. You must be aware that you and those you love are going through the various stages of loss and grief. Help is always available, and it's up to each of us to take advantage of everything that will ease any pain and suffering. If you have become too weak, you still can make peace within yourself for all the hurts, mistakes, unkind words and deeds that you may have accumulated over the years. Coming to terms with your own fallibility facilitates your transition into the next world.

Physical illness is difficult enough, but mental illness seems to be even more of a strain on us. Severe mental illness almost always alters a person's life dramatically. The signs and symptoms of mental illness are not only puzzling but also frightening to most. Often families become so upset with their mentally ill loved one because they are unable to care for him in a normal, rational way. Mental illness is still considered a stigma. Family members try to hide the shame of having a mentally ill person in the family, and often blame their loved one for bringing the disease onto himself. Such a stigma may cause families to go into denial and disassociation. It may mean institutionalizing a family member or, worse, cutting off all ties and letting him fend for himself.

Mental illness continues to be an embarrassment to our society as a whole. As I said, many of our homeless are victims of mental illness. A variety of ailments fall into this category, including schizophrenia, bipolar disorder, paranoia, depression, phobias, obsessive-compulsive behavior, post-traumatic stress syndrome, eating disorders, and even senility. Mental illness may be caused by various chemical imbalances. In some instances it may even be the result of psychic attack. Again, on a spiritual level, there are no mistakes. However, on a human level, families suffer the loss of love and affection and the normality of a loved one. They may express their grief as anger, anxiety, and even rage about something they find difficult to comprehend. A friend of mine has a cousin who suffers from schizophrenia. She's told me on numerous occasions how difficult it has been on the family. "One moment she is coherent, the next moment she flips out, like something snaps in her brain, and she becomes completely erratic and paranoid. We can't make sense out of it, and can't discuss treatment in any rational way. She's afraid of drugs because she thinks it's our way of getting rid of her. We just wish we knew what to do, but we don't. People want to help us, but we can't get her to take the first step. It's totally exhausting and exasperating. We all feel so helpless."

When any kind of a terrible illness disrupts our lives, we enter a state of ongoing grief. As with any grief, we must go through it, and look for the opportunities amidst the pain and sorrow. We have to keep our focus on a bigger picture, because all our experiences have purpose and meaning. Perhaps we must learn to love a little more.

FRIENDS IN HEAVEN

Back in 1994 I received a call from a lady by the name of Toni Sparo, who wanted a reading. The circumstances were most unusual. She told me that she was calling on behalf of her mother Gloria, who was terminally ill and supposedly had a few months to live. At first I thought that she was mistaken, or didn't understand the kind of work I did. I asked her to continue.

"My mother is afraid of death, and I thought if she could have a reading with you, it might relieve some of her anxiety and prepare her for her inevitable passing."

I was intrigued. I told Toni, "This is a first for me, but I think it is a wonderful gift to give your mother. I will be more than happy to accommodate you as soon as it is possible."

Several days later the meeting was coordinated, and at eleven o'clock the following Thursday morning, I drove to the Hollywood Hills. As I searched for the address, I came across a small pink house and noticed several people scurrying to and fro out in front. I parked my car and walked up to the door.

A medium-height woman with reddish brown hair and a nice smile greeted me.

"Come in, James," said Toni. She ushered me past the others and brought me into a huge living room.

I looked around and suddenly felt very small in comparison to the large, ornate furniture.

"Can I get you something to drink?" Toni asked.

"Just some water, please."

In a minute Toni returned with the water. She then took me by the hand and led me to another part of the house. She confided in me, "She has her good and bad moments. I think today she is pretty good, not too much pain. I told her about your coming here today, and she thinks I'm crazy. That's her reaction to mostly everything I try to do for her. She has been very angry at times. She curses everyone—her doctor, God, even the dogs."

"That's very common for someone with a terminal illness," I replied. "It just doesn't seem fair to them. They think they are going way before their time."

"Well, please forgive me if she bites your head off. She doesn't mean to."

"I'll be fine," I assured her.

We went down a hallway and entered her mother's bedroom. I was immediately hit by the antiseptic, medicinal stench that permeated the room. I felt as though I were entering a hospital ward instead of a bedroom. I looked around and quickly noticed the intricate web of tubes protruding from machines around Gloria's bed, and the sight of them gave me the creeps. By the right side of her bed were stacks of medicines, lotions, and medical supplies. There was a chair, which I figured was reserved for a live-in nurse. I also noticed a huge array of blankets, pillows, videos, a television, and photographs. Whenever I visit someone who is very ill, it seems the living don't want the sick to forget who they were, and they do whatever is necessary to make the dying extremely comfortable during their last days on earth.

"Who the heck are you?" said a strong voice emanating from a little head peeking out of the bedspread.

"My name is James. Your daughter wanted me to come and speak to you."

"Ma, I told you about James. Remember Sheila told us about him? He is the man who talks to spirits."

"Oh, geez, that's a bunch of crap," Gloria announced.

"Oh, sometimes I think life is a bunch of crap," I said deliberately in reply.

Toni looked surprised, and Gloria raised her head to get a better look at me.

After a few moments Gloria said, "Leave us alone."

Toni understood the meaning to my method, and gave me a wink as she closed the door behind her.

"I hope you didn't waste your time coming here today, Jim," she said.

I usually don't like to be referred to as Jim, but at this point that hardly seemed to matter. I sat down in the chair next to Gloria's bed and gazed at her face. She reminded me of Sophia, played by Estelle Getty, on the TV show *The Golden Girls*. Gloria could have been Sophia's twin sister, personality and all.

"What is it you do again?" Gloria asked.

"I am able to hear and see spirits who have left this earth. They share their personalities and give me messages to pass on."

"Well, there is nothing that I'd want to hear from that lot. What could they tell me anyway? Do you think they have all the answers? I don't think so!"

"You're right, they don't. They are pretty much the same in heaven as they were on the earth."

"Oh, then good luck to both of us!" she quipped.

We both chuckled. I did my best to make her feel at ease without forcing my beliefs on her. We talked for several minutes until I felt she was comfortable with me. I could tell that she wanted to believe that communication with spirit was possible. Like most, Gloria's rational side controlled the picture of the world around her. I was hoping that this day would be a little different. As we talked, I quietly meditated without her being aware of it. I began to see and hear from several people who wanted to talk to Gloria. I mentally asked them to slow down and speak one at a time, since it was impossible to get them all through at once.

"What are you staring at, Jim?" I heard Gloria say.

"Nothing much. Just some people standing behind your bed."

"Oh yeah, well, what do they want?"

I began to describe each person.

"There is a lady who I believe is your mother. She is very happy to be here, and tells me that you were her third daughter. She says Theresa is with her. She is also telling me that your father is there. She says that he has a bar of soap for you because you have been a very good girl. Do you understand this?"

I looked down and saw Gloria's face. Her jaw dropped open. I could tell she was flabbergasted.

"How do you know that? My God. Did Toni tell you that?"

I held her hand and reassured her that these were impressions from the spirit world and that they were genuine.

She took a moment to digest what she had just heard. Then she looked up at me and said, "I was the third daughter in my family. My sister Theresa died as a child, and my papa, whose name was Tony, used to own a company that made soap. When I was a little girl, he would bring bars of soap home from the factory and promise to give them to me if I behaved."

Gloria didn't know what to do with the information I had given her. I felt as though she was trying to rationalize what had just transpired. This was something she could not control. She thought about it for a few more moments before asking me to tell her what else the spirits were saying.

"There is a man standing on your left side. His hair is black with gray streaks. He gives me the name of Mack. Do you know such a person?"

"Yes, I do. Mack was my first husband. Drank himself to death."

"I also feel he smoked himself to death," I added, recognizing a cancerous condition in his lung area.

"You're right! He always had a cigarette in his mouth. How funny. Good old Mackie. How the hell are you, Mackie?"

I immediately said, "All's okay here, Glo. My ship finally came in."

I told Gloria that those were the words I heard in my head.

Gloria answered, "That was Mack's favorite expression: 'Wait till my ship comes in.' I used to say to him, 'Your ship will come in when you're dead, and a lot of good that'll do us now.'"

Gloria relayed that Mack was Toni's father, and he wasn't able to sustain a job long enough to keep the family together. "We got divorced, and I took Toni and moved back in with my mother. But we remained close and friendly. How could I ever stay mad at the father of my child? It just wasn't right. Besides, he was a nice fellow, just didn't have all the ingredients to make it as a breadwinner. I understood that."

"He wants me to tell you that heaven is waiting for you, and you have nothing to fear."

"If he is there, I sure do!" Gloria shouted back, laughing at the same time.

Mack had more information about their daughter Toni, and how proud he was of her love and caring. "He says that Toni is teaching him even now how to be compassionate."

As I was finishing up his message, another man named Joe interrupted me. "This man has ties to you from New Jersey. He wants you to know that death is very painless and very natural."

"That's easy for him to say; he died in his sleep. I could have killed him for leaving me like that," she added.

"Who was this man?" I asked Gloria.

"Oh, he was my third husband. He was a good guy, but always trying to tell me how to do things. Like anyone could tell me anything?"

I thought to myself, *No way*. I wouldn't even dare to try.

"He is mentioning gambling in Atlantic City. He said you

always had a good time, and had some friends who used to join
you there."

"Yes, that's right. Betty and Earl. I haven't thought about
them in years."

"Joe says that he must be in heaven because he has been
playing five card stud with Earl, and he's winning every game."

Gloria laughed so hard that Toni knocked on the door to
see if we were okay.

Gloria yelled back, "Couldn't be better! Go away."

She looked over and told me that Joe and Earl used to play
poker all the time. "Joe used to complain that Earl always beat
him. He hated to lose, and thought Earl had to cheat to win."

"Joe is saying how surprised he was when he came over—
that everything seemed so real and seemed to flow so naturally.
He is saying, 'Everything is timed just right here. There is
nothing out of place, and if it is, you notice right away. Nothing is coarse here. Everything is the way it is meant to be. No
one needs to worry about things because it is all taken care of
just the way heaven intended.'"

Gloria kept shaking her head and mouthing, "How nice."

Suddenly I was interrupted by a lady's voice on my right
side.

"It's a lady named Betty," I told Gloria. "She wants me to
tell you that she has a blue dress waiting for you when you
come over, and that you will be shocked at how young she
looks."

Gloria thought about what I just said. She was quiet for several minutes. "Oh, my God, that blue dress. How could you
know?"

Gloria proceeded to tell me a story. "When we were younger,
Betty and I worked together and would go out to lunch every
day. On our way we would pass this one particular dress shop
that had this beautiful blue dress in the window. I think it was

imported from Paris or Italy. Anyway, we both used to imagine how we would look all dolled up in it. We made a promise that whoever got a raise would buy the dress for the other as a token of our friendship. Isn't that something?"

Gloria stared into space as if transfixed in time.

I continued the session for another half hour, conveying some wonderful emotional details. Gloria took it all in. Somehow I knew that she was no longer afraid of death. As I got up from the side of Gloria's bed, she seemed to be in glee. I believe she had come to the realization that the illness in her body was just a brief period of time, and that she knew she had reached the end of a life well lived. There was a freshness to her face and her entire being. She looked as though she couldn't wait to see her old family and friends once again.

"Jim, thank you. Well, thank you doesn't seem to be enough, but thank you for bringing some peace to an old lady."

I began to get emotional and felt tears welling up in my eyes.

"Jim, would you do me a favor, please? I really don't want to leave my daughter Toni with a lot of problems. I want to help her. Do you think when I go, if I want to talk to her . . ." Her voice trailed off.

I knew exactly what she wanted. "I look forward to speaking to you again from whichever dimension you will be in."

Gloria thanked me, not so much in words, but with her beautiful eyes and a handshake that never seemed to end. I left that day with a feeling of fulfillment.

UPDATE

Gloria died peacefully in her sleep, as Joe said she would. That was three months after our session together. Her daughter called me, and we arranged a reading. The session began with her mother telling us how she was no longer in pain.

"I see things so much more clearly now," said Gloria. "I understand more than I did when I was on earth. And everyone is here with me. Joe, Mack, Betty, Earl, Papa, and Mama."

Gloria explained that she had learned her illness was a gift from her soul.

"I had to learn that I was not in control of every situation in my life. Getting sick was the only way I was going to learn. I have a better understanding and compassion for others. When I come back next time, I certainly will treat other people in that situation with a lot more thoughtfulness."

Toni was happy to hear her mother talk about her illness as a gift of love from spirit.

"It taught me to receive love, and to just accept things as they are," added Gloria.

I told Toni, "Your mother sees now how she tried to live your life for you, and it wasn't right. She says that you have to live each day as if it were your last. Make the most out of your life."

Gloria continued to relate that she had a new respect for life. She spoke of love not as a choice but as a reality to live by. She spoke of all the things she never did, as well as all the nice things she was able to do. She thanked her daughter for thinking enough of her to bring her comfort and joy in her final days.

"She is saying that she is definitely in heaven because she is happy, fulfilled, and loved. She is watching over you and all those she loved on earth, and those with her are taking good care of her."

Gloria's last words were, "I am even wearing that lovely blue silk dress Betty promised me."

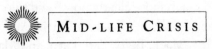

MID-LIFE CRISIS

I once asked my friend who just turned fifty, "What did you want to be when you grew up?" She replied, "Young!" I guess we all feel like that in a society that is overwhelmingly youth-oriented. We sense that we're over the hill and out to pasture by the time we're forty. I don't think I ever thought about getting old until just this past year. I was on an extensive twenty-city tour of my book, which meant lots of readings, workshops, book signings, TV, and radio shows. Almost every day I traveled to another city, and there were times when I didn't know which end was up. In between, I had to visit my father back East and help him sort out some of the things he could no longer handle. When I returned home, I had to start the writing of this book. There was my personal life, too. I guess we all feel overwhelmed to some extent, but I felt exhausted, as if I couldn't catch my breath. It was an eye-opening realization that I wasn't a kid in my twenties anymore, and I didn't have the energy I once had. It was strange to admit that my body was slowing down, and there was nothing I could do about it. Frankly, it was more than just a bad hair day; it was a rude awakening. It made me nostalgic for my youth, and the days when I had my whole life still ahead of me.

At mid-life we experience a myriad of losses essentially related to loss of youth. Some men choose to recapture this loss through fast cars and young, pretty, exciting women, and they dash off to the divorce courts. They think this will replace the regret or anxiety they may be feeling about losing their virility or sexiness. Women choose the plastic surgery and liposuction route, because they believe the myth that beauty is a statement of their self-esteem. Unfortunately, magazines, televi-

sion, and movies only keep this myth active in a woman's subconscious mind.

Mid-life also brings up a lot of uncertainty. Men may feel
that at any moment they can be terminated from their jobs, to
be replaced by younger, less costly employees. We see it happen every day in the news. Big companies "downsize" and lay
off middle-age workers to cut costs and bolster their stock
prices. Men especially have a difficult time coping with the
loss of a job. A man's self-esteem is wrapped up in his work.
Even if he has enough money to survive, there is always the
anxiety of losing everything he has worked so long and hard
for, and not being able to take care of his responsibilities. At
mid-life men also tend to reminisce a lot about the past, and
how things were simpler, less chaotic, and less pressured. They
may feel lost, abandoned, and nonessential. Then there are
the physical signs of aging for a man, and that is baldness. Men
have a terrible time with this loss. It is definitely a demoraliz-
ing lesson in self-image and self-esteem. The loss of hair to
most men signals a loss of their virility. So much value is
placed on our outer appearance that we come to identify ourselves only as what we see in the mirror.

Women, on the other hand, have very real changes at mid-
life as they go through menopause. Chemical changes in a
woman's body at this time can set off a myriad of complex issues, including loss of the ability to have children, loss of physical vitality, and loss of sexuality. Emotional issues like depression
and mood swings can cause women to feel like they are "losing
it." Menopause is a different experience for every woman. Some
women have little problems, and some have great difficulties.
Again, a lot of women are negatively programmed about growing old, and they fear becoming inconsequential. Our attitudes play an important role in how we live life. Instead of

living in dread, we can choose to believe that one only improves with age.

Besides these psychological issues about aging, women face physical issues as well. Having a hysterectomy is one. When a woman is in her twenties and just beginning to think about starting a family, the impact of a hysterectomy is devastating. Her plans for the future are dramatically altered, and she is forced to figure out how to make her life worthwhile. The scenario is quite different for a woman who is in her mid-fifties and no longer wants to bear children. I asked my fifty-two-year-old friend Erica what she thought of herself after her hysterectomy. She replied, "It wasn't pleasant. I had a lot of pain, but somehow I got through it. I would have preferred not to have it at all." Fortunately, Erica didn't experience the emotional roller-coaster ride that everyone told her to expect. However, some women may feel despondent, as they go through certain stages of grief.

Women also face the empty-nest syndrome at middle age. I think mothers definitely feel at a loss when their children leave home. I remember my friend Michelle telling me that she would pace the house every day after her daughter left home and went off to live in Paris. She said, "I would walk into her room and just stand there and stare. The thought of my little girl growing up and living far away left me cold. I felt so alone. All I could think about was the fun we once had together. It was as if I lost my best friend."

Parents feel their children are extensions of themselves, and have a hard time separating from them as they grow older. Some become fearful of their child's safety and well-being. They feel a loss of control. Part of letting children go is allowing them to be their own unique individuals. Yes, we have dreams and expectations for them, but it is truly up to them to be what they want. We must let go of our children so they can learn how to survive on their own. It is a time for grieving, but also a time for exuberance and freedom, not only for them but especially for us. With the children raised and on their own, we can take back our lives. The demands of shouldering the responsibilities of raising a family are diminished, and we have more freedom to come and go as we please. Grieving the end of this stage of life should lead us to a new optimism and enthusiasm for the next stage.

When we are young, we believe things will last forever. We never think of getting sick or old. When we reach our forties and fifties, we begin to look back and wonder where all the time went. We realize that there are things that we will never accomplish. Any dream of being on the Olympic team is for all intents and purposes over. We may have been laid off a job and believe it is too late to start over again. Or worse, we have to take a job alongside a twenty-year-old. We have to confront the inevitability of retirement, loss of income, and loss of power and prestige. We may become overwhelmed by the things we can no longer have or hope for.

The loss of youthful aspirations can cause a variety of feelings. Dissatisfaction sets in. Dreams are dead. We contemplate the should have beens and could have beens, and may have regret for our mistakes. For some, life seems like one great disappointment. We wonder what happened to our fame, fortune, and triumph. But not every life is intended to be filled in that way. We must realize that an experience is designed for our soul's development, not for earthly material gain.

We begin to think that younger people talk to us as if we have grown stupid and slow. We get angry, shaken, and a little afraid. We may feel as if we are falling apart. Any minute we think we can have a heart attack. Ultimately, we feel outdated and obsolete.

How we grieve depends on how important we perceive our

losses are. Some of us have a hard time growing up, let alone growing old. But at some point we have to let go of the youthful self-image and accept the beauty of middle age. We have to take into consideration that each age has its own unique experiences. Mid-life is a good time to take a physical, mental, and spiritual self-examination. I believe this is the time that we need to focus on spiritual priorities rather than outward appearances. Instead of speeding up to stay in step with the next generation, we need to slow down and search within for the meaningfulness in our lives. Nature is perfect. We are always at the right age. It is not the time to keep up, catch up, or hurry up to feel we are still having a life. It's not about trying to escape the terrors of aging and death, but to move ourselves forward to finding a deeper meaning to life. This doesn't mean we stop what we are doing. Rather, we must take a look at these activities to see if they are what we want, and if they are helping us appreciate ourselves and the world around us. By middle age it is only natural to question ourselves, our jobs, and our interests. At the same time, it is also normal to feel a sense of loss and lack of importance. Remember that our souls don't age. They are unchanged by any pains, adversity, or even pleasures. We may not like the wrinkles and lines we see in the mirror as we grow older, but we are still and will remain the same, real, ageless being throughout all time.

AGING

Unlike other cultures that venerate their elderly, our society discards them as yesterday's garbage. Instead of embracing their knowledge and years of rich experience, we make fun of them as a bunch of has-beens that take up space and drain our nation's economy. We give very little respect to old people. We placate them, medicate them, and eradicate them by sending them to institutions where we don't have to see or hear from them anymore. I don't think any of us want to look forward to a future where we are treated like that.

There is no denying that we live in a society that embraces youth. We are literally ashamed of getting and looking older. We are so quick to make jokes about little old ladies and dirty old men that don't match the media's picture of beauty, health, youth, and vitality. We have been programmed to believe that growing older is unacceptable, worthless, and disgusting. We have been taught to believe that being young is the only valuable commodity we have. So we spend billions of our hard-earned cash trying to preserve ourselves with creams, surgery, diet, and exercise. It is impossible not to feel the pressure of our society's attempts to keep us young.

However, the truth has been distorted. We have been taught in reverse. Instead of assessing a person from the inside out, we look at appearances and quickly jump to judgment. When we die, it does not matter what we look like, but how much we have grown as a person. In this regard, we need to take a 180-degree turn from where we are headed and look at ourselves in a completely new way. The only thing that matters is the goodness of a person's heart, and you can tell that by looking into someone's eyes.

Many of our elderly are lumped together as doddering, feeble-minded individuals who have nothing left to contribute. They feel powerless and irrelevant. When they buy into this picture of decrepitude, they begin to fall apart because that is what is expected. As more of us get older, I believe there will be some revolutionary changes in the way we treat our elderly. There are many extremely productive and creative people in their eighties, nineties, and even at one hundred. They are probably the most keenly perceptive individuals walking the planet, with a capacity to teach, enrich, and benefit younger generations.

We all hope to live to a ripe old age, but when aging brings with it loss of memory, disease, loss of income, and psychological impairment, the thought of growing old becomes less promising. Besides losing the freedom of coming and going as they please, the elderly also lose their friends. You might say, they are in a constant state of grieving. As people live longer, they find themselves without any familiar faces. Their friends and loved ones have all passed on. So besides fearing their own demise, they feel deserted and forgotten.

What many old people fear is losing control of their lives. They feel that they will become frail, fall down, and end up in a nursing home with others making their life decisions for them. I know this was a major fear of my father's, and I have reassured him that he will not be put away to die. Just knowing that he won't be discarded has empowered him. He knows he will be in control of his life. He can watch television when he wants, eat when and what he wants, and talk to his friends and family on the telephone whenever it suits him. Such little things give a person a connection to the outside world. He feels significant in his own world. He may be limited, but he still is an active member of society.

Recently I was back home visiting my father. We sat together one afternoon sharing a beautiful lunch made up of chicken salad, greens, and for him, the always present can of Coca-Cola. My dad looked at me and said in a serious tone, "Jamie, I had a dream last night of my old neighborhood. I would like to go and visit it. Do you think you might be able to drive me back there so I could see it again?"

I told him, "Sure, Pop, whatever you want."

The next day he was all dressed up in a suit and tie, which

is very rare. He had a big smile on his face as though he were a seven-year-old on Christmas morning.

"Are you ready?" he asked.

"Absolutely," I told him.

His nurse Margaret and I ushered him into the front seat of the car. He doesn't walk very well since breaking his hip during a terrible fall a year ago. Most of the time he relies on the use of a wheelchair. Anyway, once we tucked him in and secured his seat belt, he was ready for his joyride. It was exciting to see him feeling alive and happy once again. He hadn't visited his old neighborhood in over ten years, and he was naturally curious to see how it had changed. I was a little bit apprehensive for him. I knew that ten years can change a neighborhood quite a lot, and it may not bear any resemblance to what he once remembered.

We traveled up the expressway and over the Whitestone Bridge. My father directed me at every opportunity. He knew the way by heart, even if it had been ten years since his last visit. We crossed over Long Island Sound and entered the Bronx. The closer we got to his old stomping grounds, the more excited he became. He was a little boy once again, anxious to see what might await him around each new turn. We passed a park to the right, and he informed me that it was where he used to play ball with the kids from the neighborhood. It was also the place where he and his family used to enjoy a Sunday picnic. There were not many air conditioners in those days, so there was nothing better than a picnic in the park to cool off on a hot afternoon.

We continued winding down the road and finally exited the expressway. We made a left turn at the next light and were immediately stuck in a traffic jam. Slowly we inched our way westward, and as we did, I could hear my father making sounds of incredulity as he surveyed what used to be his neighborhood of Pelham Bay Park.

"I can't believe it," he remarked. "Look over there. You see that?" He pointed to an old brick public school with a wrought iron fence around it. "That's where I went to school. Nothing has changed," he exclaimed.

I was extremely happy to hear those words.

He directed me through his old neighborhood, down tree-lined streets, past attached brick homes. The neighborhood was once made up largely of Greek immigrants, and according to my father, it hadn't changed that drastically in all those years. There was a video store where his favorite bakery used to be, and a few other up-to-date changes, but for sixty years it had worn very well.

Dad had made arrangements to visit his old boyhood friend Alex earlier in the day and told Alex that we would be arriving around one in the afternoon. We parked the car in front of a yellow house that was set back from the street. The house had a front yard filled with a variety of fruit trees. It certainly stuck out among all the brick and cement, half a block from the El and all the trains roaring by every few minutes.

I went up to the front door and greeted the old man standing there with a smile on his face. I had met Alex once before at my mother's funeral. He came over to the car and gave my father a big hello. They immediately began to discuss the old days when they served in the military during World War II. I then asked Alex if he would like to join us on our tour around the old neighborhood.

Alex got in the car and immediately started to give me directions. As we circled around the blocks, we visited many familiar sights of their childhood days. We stopped at a school-yard, their old pubs, a firehouse, the neighborhood church, and a handful of houses and apartment buildings that were still standing. I listened to stories about people who were a major influence in my father's childhood. "I remember when my mother, your grandmother, got a brand-new Buick, and every time she tried to pull it out of the driveway, she would get stuck because it was just too wide to get through," my father said, smiling. "And your grandfather often fell asleep on the subway because we were the last stop, and he would spend the whole night on the train circling the Bronx."

The two friends rattled off names from the past and wondered what had happened to them. I felt transported back in time through the minds of these two men who lived during an era when friends would get together for a dance or a trip to the candy store for a soda. Their amusement was definitely not centered around a television set or a computer screen. Their dreams were about baseball or running the trains across country. Life was simpler and in some ways I think more appreciated. All that they had left were their memories of bygone days and mementos of five-cent movie tickets and yellowed baseball cards held captive in decrepit cigar boxes.

After several hours of cruising the neighborhood, I drove Alex back to his house and dropped him off. We said our good-byes, and we drove away from all that remained of lives that once were full and rich and active.

As we crossed the bridge, I asked my dad, "Was it everything you thought it would be?"

He hesitated, and eventually shook his head from side to side. "No. I thought it would be the same, but it's not. It made me feel so old. Do I look old to you?" he asked.

I said, "I think you look pretty good for seventy-seven!" Then we got into a long discussion that lasted all the way home and well into the evening. I asked him if I could include our experience in this book, and he said, "Yes, I would love it." He added, "I don't think I have very much to offer as words of advice, but if I can help others understand about getting old or how to treat those of us who are, well, then maybe it's worth it."

I asked him, "Dad, what do you think is the worst part about getting older?"

"Well, I guess it would be losing my independence. I have always been able to take care of myself, to do whatever I wanted. But now I can't. I had to give up driving ten years ago because of my bad eyesight. I now feel like an invalid. I need help with everything I do. I have to have someone pay the bills, like you when you're in town, and someone to cook food for me. I hate that. It makes me feel useless. I never had so many aches and pains as I do now. Just bending over is a pain, never mind walking or getting out of the bed to go to the bathroom. No one ever told me it would get like this."

"Do you think being old has taught you anything?" I asked.

After a few moments he said, "Oh, yes. I have had a lot of time to contemplate my life, and I keep thinking over and over again, if I only knew then what I know now. I took life for granted in many ways. One doesn't realize how precious life is. It all goes by so fast, and I don't think you have a proper perspective till you get older. When you are older, you live in your memories. They tug at the heart because you remember what you used to look like and what you were capable of doing. You wonder if you are still the same person. It really hits you hard when you see old friends, their wrinkled faces and shaky hands, and you realize what a strain life is. You are left with just yourself and your memories. I don't think of tomorrow. It doesn't mean much to me."

"What else do you think it has taught you?" I said.

"I think as one gets old, one either gets kinder or crankier. For me, I have to rely on the kindness of strangers to get through the day. I never thought that someday I wouldn't be able to get out of a car without someone's help, or even go to a store, or bathe myself. Now I have to concern myself with those things. I just took it for granted that I would do these things till the end. I wish I could do them myself, but I can't. I need help. I have a wonderful lady here who helps me. She is so kind; she takes care of me. I pay her, but it's very little compared to the amount of kindness and care she gives me. And you know something?"

"What, Dad?"

"She does it from her heart. She treats me like a king because she knows that I feel embarrassed. Her kindness has taught me what matters most in life—to treat others as you want to be treated."

What a major difference in my father's outlook! Months earlier, I would never have heard these words from his lips. Instead he would have been angry about his helpless situation. He has not only learned to understand and accept it, but also to see the fullness and goodness of the life he has left. I felt very proud of him.

"What do you think keeps you going? What keeps you alive?" I asked.

"Well, I believe that one continues to learn. The mind can always learn no matter how old you are. I myself love word games and astronomy. I read books on astronomy. Several years back, I took a class at the Hayden Planetarium. It was great. I shared some ideas with kids half my age, and we taught each other. That to me was fantastic and showed me that if you can keep the brain busy and active, you don't have to necessarily age mentally. I also think that one should keep living because there are a lot of experiences out there. I'm lucky because I never wasted time feeling sorry for myself. I figure there is always someone out there in a worse condition or situation than myself, so why should I feel sorry for me?"

"What message would you leave to your children or even other younger people about life?"

He replied, "Life is for living. I hope my children will be at least half as happy as I have been. I would like everyone to realize how short life really is and to do everything possible to make your dreams come true. Don't let anyone stand in your way because you can do whatever you set you heart to. Also, try to do your best to help people."

The conversation went on for another half hour, and then I began to feel my own age creeping up on me. I gave my dad a kiss.

"Good night, Pop. Thanks for the memories."

I'm glad my father has come to peace with growing old. So many of our elderly feel ashamed of themselves because they have to depend on others to help them get through the day. As one grows older, one certainly feels the loss of many things, not just physical energy and stamina but friends, family, dreams, desires, and purpose. Ultimately, we have to go through a myriad of perceptions, thoughts, and opinions about these losses inside ourselves. It's only normal that many feelings will surface. Like the grieving of any loss, we have to go through the process. But like my father, it's up to each of us to make peace with this part of our life. Maybe as each of us faces aging, we will make a shift in our thinking about this whole "age thing" period. Keep in mind that our souls are timeless, and the physical body is merely a shell that we voluntarily discard on the road to a glorious eternity.

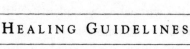

HEALING GUIDELINES

LOSING A HOME

- Allow yourself to go through the complete grieving process.
- It is always important to say good-bye to special things, such as your old home and your possessions, that you cannot take with you. Look at it as an opportunity to simplify your life, leaving room for new things to enter.
- Give away your possessions to friends or relatives with the attitude that they can furnish others with as much joy as they gave you. It will give you a pleasurable feeling to know that your possessions are in good hands.
- Do rituals that give you completion. Visit those special places one more time. Even if you cry, the tears are ones that will help you heal the necessary losses.
- Say good-bye to your house. Everything is made of energy, and there is certainly a lot of your energy in that structure. I always talk to everything when I leave: house, car, plants, and animals. I tell them how happy they have made me, and know that whoever takes my place, they, too, will get great enjoyment as well.
- Get your children involved with your move. Give them something to do, and let them make some decisions. Don't leave them out to feel deserted or rejected.
- Pace yourself during the move. Don't try to do everything in one day.
- Create a sense of yourself in your new home. Do little things that make it feel like home right away. Some flow-

ers or candles with which you identify will make a strange place more cozy and familiar.

- Connect with your new neighbors. Invite them to a housewarming party. It doesn't have to be elaborate.
- Get acquainted with your children's school through PTA or school functions.
- Keep in touch with your friends and relatives. It will ease your anxiety about feeling alienated. The telephone and e-mail are wonderful tools to help us keep in contact with loved ones.
- Do something nice for yourself. Get a massage. Sometimes getting a new hairstyle or new clothes helps open you to a new life in a new place.

COPING WITH ILLNESS

- Allow yourself to go through the complete grieving process.
- Don't try to hide your feelings.
- Be honest with yourself. Don't make mountains out of molehills.
- Clarify all communications with your doctors and health-care givers. If you don't like something, make sure you speak up for yourself. If you don't like your doctor, leave him. This is not the time to be polite to the point of hurting yourself. Having trust and faith in your health-care practitioner is as important as the medical advice itself.
- This is the time to stop blaming yourself for your illness and learn to take one day at a time in a new way. Find ways to relax and handle your stress. Visualizations, hypnosis, and prayer are probably the best ways to cope with your distress and pain.
- Get involved with a life project, which might include

reading books you have always wanted but were too busy to enjoy; reviving an old friendship; traveling, etc.

- Join a support group. There are cancer-support groups all over the country, like The Wellness Center. You can always find support through your hospital or church.

- Keep in touch with your friends and family who are positive in nature. You don't need to be around people with destructive or pessimistic behavior.

- It's okay to cry and let it out. Tears are beneficial to your body chemistry.

- Discuss your feelings and problems with your family and children when you are rested. This is a very difficult time for all of you. Allow your family to share their feelings with you, again when you are calm and not in so much pain. Only you will know when you have had enough.

- Make a living will. This gives specific directions as to how you want your health to be managed when you cannot speak for yourself.

- Put your affairs in order while you are calm and coherent. If you have possessions to leave behind, make sure everyone understands how you want them to be distributed. Make it easy for your family.

- End all turmoil with those close to you. Forgiveness is the key to letting the God Force energy flow in you.

- Embrace your life. Love yourself. You are never alone.

MID-LIFE CRISIS

- Allow yourself to go through the complete grieving process.

- Make a list of all things that make you afraid of getting older such as loss of income, sickness, feebleness, loneliness, less or no sex, and fear of death. Write everything down and then burn it. Those are your fears, but they are not your truths. Let them go.

- Make a list of all the things you still want to do in the next half of your life, such as learning a foreign language, spending time with your friends or grandchildren, volunteering for a favorite cause, taking dance lessons, learning to use the computer, or buying a vacation home. Keep this list and refer to it. Let it be a guidepost for the next half of your life.

- If you do not belong to a spiritual community, you may want to join one, or do some informal spiritual rituals such as attending a retreat.

- If you find that the religion of your youth doesn't work for you, take some classes in different spiritual disciplines, like meditation, yoga, or tai chi. Many people like A Course in Miracles or Native American practices that get them in touch with nature and animals.

- Seek out solitude. Listen to the silence. This is a way to get in touch with your true feelings. Listen to your intuition to evaluate your life and make the changes that will bring you more peace, contentment, and pleasure.

- Shut off the TV and take a walk. All those youth-oriented shows and commercials only reinforce the erroneous belief that you are inadequate and irrelevant.

- If people in your life have been destructive to you in some way, let them go with love. Practice tolerance and forgiveness.

- Use your creative energies to contribute to yourself and others.

- Find ways to balance all areas of your life. The secret to a successful life cannot be found in money or possessions, but in love for self and others and compassion for all living things.

- Meaningful activities and a good social network will lessen any mental, emotional, and physical difficulties you may be feeling as you move through middle age.

AGING

- Allow yourself to go through the complete grieving process.
- If you are able, join a seniors' center or group in your community. There are always plenty of activities, and you will be with people who have a lot to offer, and to whom you have something to offer.
- If you are having a difficult time, seek a therapist or counselor. You need to restore your own self-worth and forgive yourself and others who may have wronged you in the past.
- Assess and use available resources. You always have options. It is never too late to learn something new.
- Most of the elderly are not so much afraid of dying as the conditions of their dying. Take the necessary preparations for your death, such as authorizing a living will. Let your loved ones know how you want to be treated when the end is near. Do whatever you can to feel that you will die with dignity and in the manner in which you desire.
- Keep positive and focus on each day as it comes. Dwelling on the past and thinking negatively only lowers your immune system.
- Pay attention to others and the world around you, and your self-absorption will diminish.
- Continue to feed your mind and stimulate your senses. A day with your grandchildren, or volunteering, helps to keep you vital.
- Put your relationships in order. I am constantly being

told from spirit that healing our relationships is the
biggest lesson of all. If you have the opportunity, let go of
any ill will and make peace with anyone who has caused
problems. Forgiveness and love go hand and hand.

• Laughter is the best medicine. It is a contagious and powerful healing energy.

8

THE LOSS OF
OUR PETS

*I*n the backyard of my father's house,
etched in the corner of a brick wall, is a
faded white mark of an arrow. It points to
the side yard of the house. Above the arrow
reads: ST. MICHAEL'S PET CEMETERY. I made
that sign when I was all of seven years old,
and it has weathered the many years since.

Like any child, I had my share of ham-
sters, goldfish, and turtles. I had a very
strong attachment to them. In fact, every
day I would come home from school and sit
and talk to them in their cages or in the
aquarium. These pets were my family. I remember how I would go through the ritual
of naming each one of them and pasting a
name tag on the cage as a home address. The

first time one of my pet goldfish died, I was devastated. I asked my mother what had happened, and she told me, "It's time for the fish to go back to heaven. God has other plans for it." But I didn't understand. No matter what she said, or how she tried to console me, I still felt very hurt. I think that is why I started the cemetery. I wanted a place to go where I could sit down and talk to my friends. I recall vividly the service I would conduct when any one of my pets had died. I would light some candles and say some prayers. Then I would march to St. Michael's Cemetery in the backyard, and would place a cigar box coffin into a hole in the ground that I had dug out. I would cover it and place a cross made of two ice cream sticks marked with the name of my dead pet on top of the grave.

The cemetery was named after my brother Michael. He, too, shared an affinity for animals. He would bring home stray dogs and cats that were run over by cars. He would always bring them to the cemetery so they could have a proper burial. I used to think that if I was hit by a car and had to go back to heaven, I would want to be buried in the same way. All in all, we must have had nearly fifty to sixty graves in our backyard.

My love and respect for animals has never ceased. All animals are sacred to me, and I believe they share this earth with us to teach us many aspects about life, healing, and especially about unconditional love. Animals have become the greatest of social workers, therapists, and healers. More and more we see the use of pets to comfort the elderly or to ease the pain of those in hospitals. We have learned through scientific studies that cats can help to lower a person's blood pressure and elevate mood just by their very presence. We know all too well the importance of dogs as search and rescue animals during disaster situations. Seeing Eye dogs, hearing-aid dogs, and other dogs trained to help people with a variety of illnesses are always in constant demand.

Almost everybody's life has been touched in one way or another by an animal. In simple ways, these creatures are quick to capture our hearts. It's not uncommon for us to be drawn to the sight of a cute dog or a friendly cat, or line up in Sea World to watch dolphins and whales swim endlessly back and forth in an oversized aquarium. Children especially have a special relationship with animals. I remember all the times I visited the zoo as a child just to catch a glimpse of the magnificent lions, tigers, and elephants.

For many of us, animals play a major role in our families. Indeed, many find this member of the family a lot easier to deal with than the human members. For our animals never judge, criticize, or talk back to us. They have no hidden agendas or belief systems that can agitate or depress us. They are loyal to a fault, and no matter our moods or behaviors, they will always stay at our sides, even to the point of being abused. They are divine, extraordinary beings that demonstrate the power of giving and receiving love. For this reason we find it so much easier to connect with and trust in them. We talk to them, play with them, and travel with them. They easily become the center of attention, and we quickly form much of our daily routines around them. Having a pet is not just a part-time experience, it's a lifestyle. We always have to take our pet's well-being into consideration when making any major decisions.

The bonds we develop with our pets are extremely satisfying. As we become aware of their distinct personality traits, these bonds become even stronger. Our pets help us to express love in a totally unselfish manner. They teach us about responsibility. Like our children, our pets depend on us for shelter, food, and care when they get sick. In turn they give us loving companionship. They accept us just the way we are, which is something that we rarely find in our fast-paced world. Their loving nature brings joy and fulfillment to our lives, which helps us to feel better about ourselves. Our pets are our friends and confidantes. Whenever we feel down or upset, we can go to them for a sense of comfort and validity. By looking into their eyes, or stroking their coats, we are immediately brought back to the love that resides within. They will always remind us of who we are. We share our lives with them, and they reward us with unyielding devotion, trust, and reliability.

Animals will *always* sense our moods because they are much more aware on the psychic or intuitive levels. They rely on their innate nature to know if someone is out to hurt them or befriend them. The sixth sense is a very dominant part of their being. The next time you leave on a trip, notice how your pet will show subtle changes in behavior. Your dog or cat or bird knows that you are leaving. I always talk to my pets when I am about to take a trip and reassure them I will return.

When I was a boy, the TV show *Lassie* was very popular. I'm sure many of you remember it. Lassie certainly managed to save a lot of people from danger. She was not only smart and brave, but also gentle and loving. Lassie epotimizes the ideal in our pets. Like Lassie, our pets strive to do their best and give their all. And they ask very little in return except our care and kindness. That is why we love them as we do, and how lost we feel without them.

ANIMAL SPIRITS

One of the most common questions people ask me is: "Do animals survive death?" The answer is: "Yes! Of course they do." Animals are spirits like us. Each animal has a complete soul personality and a distinct divine purpose. Much like human death, when the physical body can no longer carry the spirit, the spirit of an animal is released and goes into the spiritual dimensions. Many spirits have shared with me that there is a "keeper of the animals," a being that oversees them in the spiritual world. It seems that most animals serve where they are needed most, and where they can help other spirits of the human kind. It is quite common for a pet to be among those who greet departed loved ones at the time of their passing into spirit, especially if the love bonds were exceptionally strong.

The other most common question I am asked is, "Can they communicate from spirit?" And the answer again is a resounding "Yes!" I have brought through hundreds of messages from the animal kingdom. The loving energy that accompanies this transmission is nothing less than pure bliss and is far superior to most of the communication I have experienced. Unlike humans', animal energy is not polluted by earthly judgments and opinions, and usually comes through with adoration, gratitude, and love.

I have often felt that the animal kingdom works together with the human kingdom in a divine plan. This may manifest in ways that we cannot fully understand from our present vantage point. But I do believe that animal consciousness does its part to help us to connect to the truth of that perfect love from which we all originate. I speak not only of the obvious actions that have already been described, but in psychic ways as well. I believe that animals are easily impressed by spirit. I have known of times when animals have interfaced with humans at the moment of death or shortly thereafter. They are actually conduits for meaningful signs and messages from the spirit world.

For instance, after someone dies, it is very common to have an experience with an animal that immediately causes us to think of our loved one. Some of these occurrences are more blatant than others. I remember this kind of experience when my mother passed over. During the funeral service, the priest in his eulogy asked us to see our mother's spirit as one held captive in her body much like a caterpillar in its cocoon. At death, he said, the spirit is free to ascend to heaven much like the emerging butterfly is free to soar into the sky. This was a reassuring thought for my family, and even though I do this kind of work all the time, it was a gentle reminder to me as well. It was something I needed to hear.

Since that eulogy my siblings and I have often reminded each other of the butterfly story. For years after my mother's death, if we happened to see butterflies appear at an anniversary or birthday celebration, we would think it was Mom coming to join us. This was understandable when these events occurred in the spring, summer, or fall, but on several occasions butterflies appeared in winter months as well. My rational mind tried to find an explanation for such demonstrations, but damned if I could find one. My siblings insisted that the butterfly was my mother, or that she was influencing it. I thought it was a beautiful sentiment but purely symbolic.

During a trip to Brazil I came to believe that the butterfly was something more than merely a symbolic gesture. I had brought a group of people on a spiritual retreat in which we visited several psychic centers around the country. These centers housed healers and mediums of all types, and the group was able to take part in some incredible healing demonstrations. When we had finished our week of sacred intimacy, we took a trip to a spectacular waterfall in the southern part of Brazil. I went off by myself and sat under a tree where I did a closing meditation on behalf of my group. I thanked the spirit world for all the life-altering experiences that everyone had encountered during the past week. While in meditation, my mother came to me clairaudiently and told me that she was proud of my helping so many people to gain enlightenment. I could hear her voice as she told me that she was always with me. "Just look around, James, and accept it" were her words. I thanked her and blessed her and told her, "I know you're around, Mom." As I opened my eyes, a beautiful orange and blue butterfly rested in the open palm of my right hand. Tears began to roll down my face. I knew from that moment on, I would never question the appearance of a butterfly again. It was my mother's way of giving me confirmation that she was always guiding and protecting me.

SPENCER, OUR HERO

I don't think we humans quite understand the extraordinary intelligence and courage of our animals. I know we have heard stories of animals risking their lives, or beating the odds and traveling long distances to reunite with a beloved owner. Many animals serve as our guardians. They seem to be plugged into our welfare on many levels. I believe that some animals have a specific service on this earth as life-saving angels sent from God to keep us on our spiritual path. This was particularly expressed in the following story about a remarkable pet.

In the middle of a public demonstration, as I was giving a message to a lady named Corey from her dear father who had recently passed, an image of a big black dog running toward me appeared in my mind. The image changed so quickly that I could barely get the description out of my mouth.

"I just got this funny image. Your father is showing me a dog. It looks like a black German shepherd. Did he own this animal? It appears to be running all around him."

"No," Corey answered.

Unsure of what I was getting, I had to give her several more details before she understood the image to which I referred.

"This animal is showing me a left eye. I feel the animal had a problem with his left eye. I see blood in the socket. It could be cataracts."

Corey's facial expression changed completely. Her eyes became as wide as saucers. She covered her mouth with both hands and gasped.

"Oh, my God. Yes!" she exclaimed.

"The dog wants you to know he can see again and is thanking you for helping him with his eye."

"Yes. I brought him to the vet. Oh, my God," she exclaimed once again.

Then she started to cry, and an audience member next to her stood up to help her. Corey was in a bit of a shock.

She uttered, "It's Spencer! It's Spencer! I know him. It's my dog, Spencer!"

Corey burst into tears. We had to wait a few minutes until she was able to compose herself. The audience member stood by to console her. When I felt she was comfortable, I continued.

"This dog brings you so much love. I feel this dog was very special."

At that moment the spirit dog jumped in front of her and started to lick her face.

"He wants to kiss you," I said.

The whole audience intoned an enormous "Ah."

"I am seeing a ribbon around the dog's neck. It looks like a gold medal attached to a purple ribbon. I feel this dog was more than just a family dog. He wants me to tell you that he was sent to be your protector."

Corey just nodded her head affirmatively. As she began to calm down, a smile appeared on her face in the midst of her tears. "I just can't believe it's Spencer."

Then I was given the impression of a name.

"Do you know someone by the name of Tracey? I believe the name is Tracey."

"Yes, I do. That's my daughter. But she is here on earth; she hasn't died."

"Funny, I am seeing the name Tracey spelled out in front of this dog. I am also feeling smoke, like I am choked up and have trouble breathing."

Not sure what this meant, I mistakenly misinterpreted the image. "Did your father have trouble breathing, because that is what I am picking up."

"No, he didn't die that way. But I think I understand what you're getting at, James. Please go on. I want to hear more."

"Well, I don't know why, but I feel that this dog wants to be with Tracey or wants to be known to her. Does that make sense?" I asked.

"Yes, James. It does."

The reading went on for several minutes more as Corey's father had additional information to give her. He wanted her to assure various members of the family that he was no longer suffering. "He is saying that he feels full of life now that he is out of his physical shell."

After the workshop, Corey came up to me privately and told me, "Everything you said makes so much sense to me now." She then apologized for not realizing at the time what I was telling her because it all seemed so inconceivable.

She went on to say, "When I was first married, Tom, my husband, and I wanted to get a dog. We weren't sure if we wanted to go through a breeder or find one at the pound. Anyway, we went to the pound and fell in love with this little wire-haired terrier mutt. But we went home to think about it some more. When we returned two days later, the little mutt was gone. They had already found her a home. We were a little down about it. On our way out of the pound, we saw this black German shepherd in the last cage on the left. He was a bit older than the rest of the dogs. As we walked by, he came to the front of the cage and stared at me. I bent down to pat him, and he began to lick my hand like he had known me forever. Tom and I decided that even though we were thinking of a much smaller and younger dog, there was something about this dog that we found very endearing and comforting.

"Anyway, we took him home and named him Spencer. He quickly became one of the family. Several months later, I found out I was pregnant. Spencer would follow me everywhere I went, as if he was taking care of me because of my condition. It wasn't until I was about to have my baby that we truly found out just how special Spencer was. Tom had been working the graveyard shift. One night just before Tom left for work, Spencer seemed very nervous and agitated. He wouldn't sit down, but instead would pace back and forth. In the middle of the night, I got up to get a glass of water, and on my way to the kitchen, I tripped over a box in the middle of the floor. I fell down and was in a lot of pain, and then I began to bleed. The last thing I remember was the sound of Spencer's barking. Somehow he had gotten out, and had begun barking his head off in the front of the house. His barking awakened my next-door neighbor Judy, who came over and found me lying on the floor. To make a long story short, she called the paramedics, and they came and took me to the hospital. I gave birth to a healthy daughter, Tracey, but the doctor said that if I had not gotten to him in time, I could have lost her!

"And then, within the first year after Tracey's birth, Tom and I were awakened my Spencer's pulling at our blankets with his teeth. The moment we awakened, he barked and ran into the baby's room. When we got there, we saw that our daughter had stopped breathing and was turning blue. Tom quickly called 911, and I gave her mouth-to-mouth, and she revived. If it wasn't for Spencer, she might not have been here today."

UPDATE

Spencer lived with Corey, Tom, and Tracey another four years before he passed away. Corey said that he had developed a very close relationship with her daughter, who is now five years old. "He would sleep at her side every night, and if there was anything ever wrong with her, he would bark incessantly to awaken us. It's no wonder he wanted to make himself known to her. Spencer definitely was our hero, and we owe him everything. We miss him very much."

SKYLARK

Many times I have had the opportunity to bring through messages from animals that express how little habits or the special things that their caretakers did made them happy. The following communication is one that was filled with this kind of appreciation.

Byron and Joanne Baker had lost their son Brian to leukemia at the age of eight years old. In the two years that followed, they, along with their daughter Marlene, or Marlee as she was called, attempted to reach him. When Brian came through during our reading together, he comforted his family with a wonderful message of optimism and joy.

I could hear excitement in his message as he relayed it to me. "He is saying that he was not in pain when he died, and now that he's in heaven, he can have all the ice cream he wants."

Brian continued to say that he was in a type of school with other children and had many, many friends.

I said, "He wants to know why you are so sad if he is so happy."

Brian further went on to tell his parents that a lady called "Ta Ta" was taking care of him.

His mother replied, "That is my great-aunt Tamara. She died ten years ago."

When I thought the reading was filled with excellent evidence and didn't expect much more, Brian still had something to say that surprised everyone.

"Brian wants you to know something, Marlee. He is saying that Ta Ta has taken him to feed Skylark, and that he got to pet her."

Immediately Marlee began to cry. She placed her hands up to her face.

In my mind's eye, I began to receive an impression of a huge horse.

"I am seeing a gray horse standing in front of me. It has a white spot on its head and is shaking its head up and down. Is this Skylark?"

"Yes," said Marlee.

"This might seem strange to you, Marlee, but I am being given the impression from this horse that it became very feverish before it died, and that you and your father called many different vets to get help."

"Yes, that's right. She supposedly had a deadly sort of virus," replied the young girl.

The father chimed in, "We tried all the vets throughout New England to find out what she was ailing from. So many came to help but could do nothing for her."

Joanne curiously asked, "You mentioned my son with the horse. How is that possible?"

It was a typical question that I am often asked when animals surface in a reading.

I explained, "Well, in the heaven worlds, you are able to see loved ones and animals which you once knew. Brian was obviously brought to the animal for a reason. Perhaps to make the boy feel more at home. Also, animals usually are in an environment that suits them. In Skylark's case, this would probably be a pasture or a field of green."

"Skylark loved riding in the meadows," added Marlee.

I continued with the reading. "This animal is giving me a very strong personality. But I am also getting that this horse would not like everyone. She was very picky about people."

I looked over to the group for some validation.

They all sat there somewhat shocked and at the same time somewhat amused.

Joanne answered, "Oh, my, yes, that's very true. Very true! If Skylark didn't like someone, she would turn around and walk away. We could usually tell the character of a person just by watching Skylark's behavior."

"Marlee, Skylark is giving me the impression that you slept in her stall when she was ill. She wants you to know that she really appreciated your caring and love."

Marlee began to cry again, and could only nod in understanding.

I continued receiving thoughts and visions from this impressive animal. She presented a beautifully strong energy of love with each new idea.

"Wow, this is interesting. I think you must know that this horse comes to see you in the evening. She is giving me the impression that you still have her blanket. It is in the bedroom. Do you understand this?" I asked Marlee.

Once again everyone looked surprised.

Marlee looked over at her parents, then back at me, and

said, "Yes, I have the blanket. It's at the bottom of my bed. I look at it every day and think of Skylark. That's amazing!"

"Skylark is relaying to me that you were best friends. She tried to do her best with the jumps. She really tried hard. Do you understand?"

This time Byron was amazed.

"Skylark was a strong, competitive horse," he said.

Then Marlee finished his sentence. "We were in horse shows together. We even won some awards."

"Some awards? You have over twenty of them from all over the country," proudly interrupted her mother.

I was very happy that Marlee's devoted animal had come through.

"Will I see her again?" Marlee asked.

"Of course you will," I replied. "Throughout your life Skylark will be around you as she was on earth, and when it is your time to go home to spirit, she will be there to welcome you. One of the wonderful things about our animals is that they are with us for as long as we need them."

And as soon as I told her that, I had another flash of Skylark nodding her head up and down, whinnying. "I think Skylark agrees with me."

Suddenly I saw a blue ribbon falling from a wall. I asked the family if this had any significance.

"Yes," Marlee responded. "A ribbon fell off the wall this morning. It was right above my bed. It was a blue ribbon, the last award I won with Skylark before she died. It's funny you mentioned it, because after that happened this morning, I could have sworn I felt Skylark's silky mane in my hands."

UPDATE

The Baker family's life seems to have moved forward since their time with me. A reading doesn't necessarily make anyone's pain go away. Instead, it offers a new and distinct revelation about life after death. In the meantime, Marlee has begun high school and has decided to end her competitive riding career. She said to me that she no longer desires to have another horse. "I keep a journal now, and write about my thoughts and dreams." One of her favorite entries is the one about Skylark. "I dream of us riding together through a brilliant meadow of flowers of every color of the rainbow. We're jumping over fences and flying through the air. I know that we will always be together."

PET MEMORIES

Over the years I have received many letters from people who want to express their love for a family pet. These letters are filled with appreciation for an animal that helped them in some way to love life a little more or assisted them in healing themselves. Some of these transmissions were so beautiful and heartfelt that I wanted to bring them to you so that you, too, could share in these unique and loving moments. These are your stories.

Annie

For eight years I had a cockatiel bird named Annie. She was a marvelous companion and a source of great inspiration and joy for me. Annie was white with a bright yellow crown and yellow-tipped wings and tail. She had these two rosy orange cheeks which made her appearance vibrant and distinct. She knew she looked good, and she was proud enough to show off.

At the time, I lived quite close to the beach, and I used to take Annie for walks, like other people would walk their dogs. Only Annie would perch on my shoulder instead of being tethered on a leash. Having always loved and respected the freedom and grace of birds in flight, I never clipped Annie's wings. I would put her on my shoulder, and out the door we'd go. I always knew Annie chose to be with me because she could certainly fly away anytime she wanted. When we were halfway between the sand and the surf, I would raise my index finger so Annie could step down. She would always playfully nip at it, as if to let me know she was in charge. Her bite was an affectionate gesture and part of our bonding together. She would stand proudly on my finger, and in one delirious moment, I'd throw caution to the wind and wave her into flight. She would take off with such abandonment after being in a cage all day. It was such a sight to see! People on the beach would stop whatever they were doing and stare at her in wonder. She was a little bird, but she flew in giant circles over the shore until she was ready to return. She would then pinpoint her landing directly on my shoulder. I would scratch her head to compliment her excellent arrival, and once again she would nibble at my index finger. This seemed to signify Annie's independence, genuine love, and gratitude. Our walks together would always be at sunset, because we both seemed to love that time of day best of all. Annie was my best friend and companion through some very trying times. She always managed to bring so much joy into my life just when I needed it the most. When she died, I was heartbroken.

I felt a huge void inside myself that left me incon-
solable.

Fourteen years after Annie's death, I found myself
on a snorkeling trip off a little island near Bora Bora in
Tahiti. I stepped into the beautiful turquoise waters at
this dreamy vacation spot and headed out toward a reef.
I quickly encountered a menagerie of multicolored
tropical fish. A bright yellow fish seemed to head
straight toward me. Somehow I thought it wanted to
welcome me to the sea and show me its home. When
I took a closer look at it, I noticed two orange spots on
each of its gills. When I put my hand out to touch it,
it took a little nibble at my index finger. Just then a realization flooded my mind as memories of Annie returned. I thought, *Could this be my bird as this exquisite
fish?* Annie had always loved the ocean. She could
certainly be as free as a bird in the vast blue waters of
this lovely island paradise. It was at that moment that
I understood that love for a pet never dies. It lives
within our hearts forever. I know Annie will always be
in mine.

—Lindy Carroll
Hermosa Beach, California

Chester the Cat

I have always lived with cats; somehow cats and I
have always been drawn to each other. I think it is because we share a unique understanding and respect for
one another. Four years ago a beautiful chestnut brown-
haired cat found its way to my doorstep. It seemed obvious that this cat had not been taken care of and was
in dire need of food and water. It certainly came to the
right home. Perhaps it knew I was partial to cats. I im-

mediately prepared a bowl of food and left it on the porch. I didn't press the cat to come inside. I knew it would eventually make up its own mind whether to stay or leave.

After a few weeks, the cat began to come into the house and, before I knew it, took over. I named him Chester because of his beautiful coloring. It didn't take long for Chester to find the most comfortable chair in the house and make it his own. Chester and I immediately became best of friends. Surprisingly, he got along with the rest of the cats in the household as well. Like the other cats, he got into a daily routine. He would exit the cat door at night and return every morning for his breakfast. One morning Chester didn't return. I waited all day and all night for him, but he never appeared. Somehow I knew he wasn't coming back, and I was heartbroken. As time passed, I often wondered, *Whatever happened to dear Chester?*

Then one day, as I was taking a walk around the neighborhood, I spotted a cat sleeping on a porch. He had the same chestnut coloring as Chester. As I got closer I realized it was Chester! I called his name, and he came running over and brushed up against me, purring. I was so happy to see him again. As I bent down to pet him, I heard a woman's voice call out, "Smoky! Come here, Smoky." The cat immediately turned and walked toward the voice. I looked up and saw an elderly lady standing at the porch door. I went over to introduce myself and tell her about Chester. She invited me inside for a cup of tea.

As we sat in the kitchen, the woman told me how the cat had appeared out of nowhere on her doorstep several months earlier. She said, "He insisted on staying." She then said that I was welcome to take him back home with me. I was overjoyed. But when I picked Chester up to take him home, he leaped out of my arms. At that moment we looked into each other's eyes. I could feel his energy, and knew that he loved me, but he seemed to convey that he had something to do that was more important. I knew then that he wasn't mine to keep. I kissed him good-bye on the top of his head and told the lady, "It's all right. This is his home now. He should stay with you." A smile came to her face. I could tell she was extremely relieved and very grateful to keep her little friend. As I left, she thanked me over and over again.

About six months later, I happened to run into the same lady in the supermarket. I asked about Chester. She relayed that soon after our meeting, her husband had been diagnosed with cancer and had passed away. I was shocked to hear the news and gave her my sympathy. She told me that throughout her husband's illness, Chester stayed on her husband's bed every day to keep him calm and peaceful. She felt the cat had been a godsend. "I don't know what I would have done without him." We said our good-byes, and I promised to drop by now and then for a cup of tea. As I walked away, I realized that Chester had indeed something important to do. It was as if he was an angel sent from heaven to comfort this woman. I was so glad that he was there when she needed him the most, and so happy that he had been a part of my life, too.

—Carol Carpenter
Reseda, California

Nellie and Old Mother Hen

I have been a chicken farmer for well over thirty-five years, and have had my share of pets and animals. I know that they are a gift for us while we are here on earth. I hope that when my time comes, I will be greeted in heaven by all the farm animals and pets that have been a part of my life and have made it so enjoyable.

We always have had several ducks and geese, and I thought I had seen it all, but this one incident stood out in particular. About five years ago we had a white Pekin duck named Nellie. She quickly became a favorite of our grandchildren. They would feed her every day, and let her float with them in their little plastic pool. During Easter they would tie a bow around her neck and call her the Easter Duck. As the kids went on their Easter egg hunt, she would follow them around the farm, making quite a clamor with her quacking. Nellie was not an ordinary duck; she was really a member of the family. It wasn't unusual to find her in the kitchen during mealtimes. My wife would put her food in a bowl, and she would peck at it, making this terrible racket as her bill rapped the plate. That spring Nellie laid several eggs in the barn. She didn't start to nest yet, but she kept those eggs completely covered and out of sight.

One day a delivery truck came up our driveway. Unfortunately, the driver couldn't see Nellie, who accidentally got in the way. He ran over her and killed her instantly. It was a tragedy. At first we were in a state of shock. Everyone was so heartbroken, especially our grandchildren. They took it very badly. My wife Helen and I didn't know what to do with Nellie's eggs, but we wanted to keep her offspring alive if possible. Helen came up with a plan to place the eggs under one of the hens in the chicken house. It was a gamble. We had to hope that we could move the eggs without disturbing them too much. Even the slightest shake would be the end for the embryos. Then we had to hope that our hen wouldn't push the trespassers out of her nest.

The plan somehow miraculously worked. Thirty days later the eggs hatched, and out came three adorable little ducklings. Although they looked unlike any of the other little chicks we had running around, they immediately connected to the hen as their mother, and she adopted them as well. It was most unusual, but such a wonderful sight to see.

The next day the mother hen left the coop followed by her ducklings. As they passed a large puddle of rain runoff in the back of the farm, the ducklings headed straight for the water and began to paddle around. The hen went berserk and began to squawk at the top of her lungs. My wife and I ran out of the house to find out what all the commotion was about. The hen kept circling around the ducklings, screeching for the chicks to get out. The poor little ducklings were so confused. It was just their instinct to go into the water. We quickly scooped them out to stop the hen from squawking. She then checked over each one completely to make sure it was okay.

The ducklings have grown up and are full-fledged ducks. They follow our grandchildren around the farm just like Nellie used to do. And they still stay close to the henhouse and their surrogate mother. When my wife and I look at those ducks, we know that Nellie would have been proud of them. We hung her bow up in the henhouse as a reminder of Nellie the Easter Duck and the mother hen who saved her chicks.

—Benson Whittier
Aberdeen, Texas

GRIEVING FOR A PET

A pet's loss is never easy to accept, and we grieve its loss just as we would the death of a loved one. When your pet makes the transition from this world to spirit, you may feel great distress as you go through the various stages of grief. You may feel shock, anger, denial, guilt, sadness, and loneliness. You must express your feelings because repressing them can make the grieving process last that much longer. Do not let anyone else convince you that "it was just an animal." The reality is that the friend with whom you shared so much is gone, and it is normal to experience emotional upheaval. The stability of your routine has been drastically altered, and you must rearrange your pattern of behavior. Your hurt and grief are very real. Never let anyone belittle, begrudge, or negate your feelings.

Remember that each person, including every family member, will react differently to the situation, so you can never expect someone to behave the way you think he or she should. People handle loss in different ways.

It is not surprising that some people feel guilty when a pet dies. They feel they could have done something to prevent it. We all feel so helpless when a pet gets old or sick. We wish our animals could talk to us and tell us where it hurts. I remember that at the time of my divorce, I had to find new homes for my dogs. In truth, it was harder to part from them than it was my wife. I went through severe separation anxiety. Fortunately, I was able to place them with caring families, and I knew they would be cherished and loved. Nevertheless, I still felt a lot of grief.

Grieving the loss of a pet can be even more traumatic if you live alone and your pet was an intimate part of your love and caring. Crying over your dead pet is natural. Let your feelings out; it will help you to begin the process of grief.

It is also enormously beneficial to share your feelings with family members and friends who can give you much needed support. Some people may not be very sensitive to your grief. Find supportive pet lovers who understand how you are feeling. As surprising as it may seem, there are hundreds of pet grief support groups. Also, do not be influenced by a suggestion to get another pet right away. You need to grieve for your pet and not repress your sadness by substituting another pet in its place too quickly to make you feel better.

Parents have to explain the death of a pet to their children as well. This can be very confusing and upsetting for them, especially if this is the first time they have confronted a death. It may be difficult to explain to young children about the process of dying and death, but you must do the best you can to let your child know that his or her pet is not coming back. You must assist them in some way to express all of their feelings and at the same time point out that feelings are different for everyone and will vary from moment to moment. They should not expect to feel only sad, but may feel alone and angry. Some children get angry because they don't understand why their pet is gone. Your children will look up to you for guidance. Use this time as an opportunity to teach them about life and death. Make sure to let them know that your pet's passing is a part of life. Reassure them that the pet is safe. Tell your children that as time passes, they will feel better and be happy once again.

I remember a friend of mine telling me a story about her favorite cat. She came home one evening after work and found a note posted on her front door. Her beautiful all-white, long-haired kitty had gotten out of the house and was run over by an automobile. The local animal control officer left a note to inform her of its demise. She told me, "I walked into my apartment and began to sob uncontrollably. The hard part was still to come. I had to pick up my little girl at the baby-sitter's and tell her that our beloved Queenie was dead. I knew it was going to be very upsetting for her. I had to convince my daughter that it was nobody's fault." The two of them spent that evening sharing memories, expressing grief, and crying for their beloved friend. "The next day my daughter said to me, 'Mom, I can't cry anymore. It hurts too much. Let's not talk about the cat for a while until we feel better.' I thought that was probably the wisest thing we could do at the time. Thank God our other two cats were safe and well and by our sides." My friend honored her child's wishes and supported her child's feelings. Instead of brushing them aside as trivial or unimportant, she allowed her daughter to grieve in her own way. It's important that we give everyone in the family the space he or she needs to grieve.

Many people express their love for their animal by having a memorial service for it. You can bury your pet in your backyard and mark its place, as my brother and I used to do. You can have your children draw a picture or write a story about your pet. You can collect pictures of your pet and store them in a scrapbook as a remembrance. Whatever feels right to you is really okay. Some people want an even more formal affair that can be arranged through various organizations that specialize in pet services.

Grieving for a pet is a process. Remember that you are in a vulnerable state, and each day will be different from the next. Take one day at a time. Eventually the void you feel will slowly fill with loving memories of times shared with your animal. You may remember happy or humorous moments, and that is the way it should be. When you reminisce, enjoy the memory. Laugh again. Experience it as if you were still there, and then bring those feelings into your present consciousness. Remember that there is no set time period for grieving. You should not feel ashamed or angry with yourself for not being able to get over it right away. As you readjust your daily routine, the sadness and grief will subside. At that point you may be ready to adopt another friend and companion and share your love with a new pet.

EUTHANASIA

I have often been asked by people who had to put their animal "to sleep" if they did the right thing. They are burdened by guilt, and many have a hard time forgiving themselves over this final act. The decision is never an easy one and is always accompanied by a variety of emotions.

There is nothing that I could say to tell an individual that euthanasia is a right or wrong choice. From a personal standpoint, I always say that it depends on the motivation behind the act. Was this decision made out of love and caring for the health of the animal? Were you demonstrating an act of kindness because the animal was in pain or the quality of its life would be compromised? Every individual who owns an animal will have to go deep within his or her heart to feel what is right for the animal. Remember that the animal has a soul, and its soul can never be harmed.

Many people have also asked me, "Is euthanasia a painful process?" I am not a professional veterinarian, so one should check with an appropriate source. In researching this chapter, the veterinarians I contacted informed me that euthanasia is not a painful process. Usually a pain reliever is administered, and the animal falls into a deep sleep as its spirit passes out of its physical shell.

According to Bruce Fogle, DVM, author of *Pets and Their People*, the following reasons are most appropriate for ending a pet's life:

1. Overwhelming physical injury
2. Irreversible disease that has progressed to a point where distress or discomfort cannot be controlled
3. Old-age wear and tear that permanently affects the quality of life
4. Physical injury or disease resulting in permanent loss of control of body functions
5. Aggressiveness with risk to children, owners, or others
6. The carrying of untreatable disease that is dangerous or fatal to humans

If you decide that euthanasia is necessary for your animal, gather an emotional-support team around you. Let them know that you will need their love, care, and help at some point. This might include accompanying you to the vet or even helping you to organize a memorial service. Remember, no one knows, not even you, how and to what degree you will be affected. Therefore, make sure to have a safety net of people close by. It is amazing how much we go through to ensure that our pet is out of pain and trauma, but how little we help ourselves with our own stress and turmoil. The only one who can make this decision is you. Remember that your loving pet will always be around you in spirit, and when it is your turn to pass, you will once again experience the bountiful and reassuring love connection you and your pet once shared on earth.

HEALING GUIDELINES

- Allow yourself to go through the complete grieving process.
- Do not deny your feelings. You have lost a significant partner in your life, and this is your time to express your emotions. Crying is normal. Share your feelings with family members. Be aware of your children's feelings as well.
- Say good-bye to your pet. Perhaps you want a memorial service. It could be a simple candle lighting and a prayer. Or it could be more elaborate with poems, pictures, and pet toys, etc. Do what works best for you and your family. As with any grieving, it is important to have some sort of closure.
- Join a pet support or bereavement group and share your sorrow and grief. Other pet owners will understand your situation and can be a very solid sounding board. Usually your vet will have information about these pet support groups. You can also go on the Internet. There are many websites dedicated to pet loss and grief.
- Help your children by listening to and encouraging their feelings about the animal. Never inhibit a child's feelings or force him or her to get over it. If your children are very young, have them draw pictures about how they feel and encourage them to discuss all the characteristics they loved about their pet.
- Inform your child's teacher about the loss. It is normal for a child to express the emotions related to grief during school time. It would be hard for the teacher to properly assess a child's moods if she is unaware of the situation.
- Establish new daily routines while you are grieving. Do

something different that takes the place of the routine you had with your pet, or change the order of how you do things. This could even include changing the furniture around in your house or doing activities at different times of the day.

- Dedicate something in your pet's name to an organization, such as having a tree or rosebush planted as a memorial. Perhaps you may want to have a plaque engraved with your pet's name and a special inscription. You can donate to an animal organization in your pet's name as well.
- Put away your pet toys, food, bed, etc. Having these things around may only stir your emotions and keep you sad and depressed.
- Make a list of all the wonderful attributes your pet had. What has this loving companion taught you about life and about yourself? How have you changed because of your pet?
- If you feel you want to have a new animal, make a list of all the attributes you want from this new animal. What would you change about yourself when sharing life with a new animal?
- Realize how lucky and blessed you were to have shared such a unique experience with another living being and how much love there was between you.
- Each day, try to do one positive thing for yourself.
- This is a time for self-understanding and self-love. As you go through your mourning process, take whatever time out of your daily activities that you can. I know many people who have taken time off from work when a pet has died.

The Rainbow Bridge

By the edge of a woods, at the foot of a hill,
Is a lush, green meadow where time stands still.
Where the friends of man and woman do run,
When their time on earth is over and done.
For here, between this world and the next,
Is a place where each beloved creature finds rest.
On this golden land, they wait and they play,
Till the Rainbow Bridge they cross over one day.
No more do they suffer, in pain or in sadness,
For here they are whole, their lives filled with gladness.
Their limbs are restored, their health renewed.
Their bodies have healed, with strength imbued.
They romp through the grass, without even a care,
Until one day they start, and sniff at the air.
All ears prick forward, eyes dart front and back,
Then all of a sudden, one breaks from the pack.
For just at that instant, their eyes have met;
Together again, both person and pet.
So they run to each other, these friends from long past,
The time of their parting is over at last.
The sadness they felt while they were apart,
Has turned into joy once more in each heart.
They embrace with a love that will last forever,
And then, side-by-side, they cross over together.

—*Steve and Diane Bodofsky*

PART IV

Reclaiming Your Life

9

SELF HARMONY

*G*rieving in a way represents the final stages of one part of our lives, and at the same time signals the start of a new beginning. Grieving allows us to cleanse ourselves so that we can start a new part of our journey refreshed, energized, and a little bit wiser. The Universe has provided each one of us with all the necessary equipment to enable us to get through and over our losses.

Loss in any form, like any obstacle we encounter in life, represents real opportunity for each of us to challenge ourselves and to grow spiritually. Recognizing the opportunity will allow us to approach the experience as a voyage of discovery. It is a very special voyage that takes us into ourselves and allows us to see ourselves in a way that we have never seen before. We cannot help but be transformed.

By no means am I diminishing the pain and suffering that we physically and emotionally experience, but once we can accept that it is all part of the human experience, we can begin to place things in their proper perspective. What I am attempting to impart to each of you is that human loss is just a temporary separation of spiritual beings that have shared the physical experience together. As I have repeated so many times, and something that I believe with all my heart, the bonds of love shared in the physical are the bonds that remain alive forever.

If your belief system embraces eternal life as well as the certainty that you will see your loved ones again, and that they are always with you, then you will be able to renew your commitment to life. Just remember it is not the end, it is the beginning.

This chapter is about reclaiming your life as you process your grief. With that in mind, I have created meditations and exercises that will help you to express your feelings, as well as to let go of unwanted attitudes and behavior. As you gain new awareness, you will come to a realization that you will indeed survive your grief.

HEALING REMINDERS

I find that whenever I am thrown into an unexpected tailspin from a loss, I must bring myself back to spiritual basics. I must remind myself that I am in charge of my life, and that only I have the power to choose my next step. Will I react to a situation or use it to "act" in a new way or with a new attitude? Often things occur so quickly, we barely have time to think.

That is when we must remind ourselves of some very basic truths.

In order to move beyond your grief and sorrow and to feel reconnected to your true self, you will have to change some of your negative attitudes about life into ones of joy and happiness. This is the only way you will be able to make the most of your future experiences. I hope the ideas and affirmations listed below will help you gain the same inspiration and encouragement that I have received from them.

1. Love never dies.
2. Fear is an illusion. Only love is real.
3. Count every moment as a blessing.
4. Tears are cleansing the hurt and opening my heart to a happier future.
5. As I release my grief, all fear, bitterness, and pain dissolve from around my heart, and I discover the joy of life.
6. Every thought is creating my future.
7. From every drop of rain, a rainbow is born.
8. Today's losses are tomorrow's gains.
9. A wise person never stops learning.
10. When opportunity knocks at my door, I am ready to open to new possibilites.
11. I value every moment with the ones I love, and I let them know what's in my heart.
12. I can make a choice to stay centered in the midst of confusion.
13. Earth is the schoolroom, and we are the students. We all take different courses and graduate at different times.
14. I cannot control the Universe, but I can control myself.
15. Make an effort to take part in the dance of life.
16. It is good to share a tear, a laugh, a sigh with a friend. We are both being healed in our love.

17. Instead of judging myself or someone else, I think lov-
    ing thoughts.
18. Give without any expectation in return.
19. Nothing is lost; something is being transformed.
20. I accept love as the healing power in my life.

METAPHYSICAL TERMS

Throughout the following meditations and exercises I refer
to various metaphysical phrases and terms that you will need to
understand. By setting up your environment with balance and
harmony, your spiritual work will be that much more satisfying.

SPACE

As you do these exercises, it is very important that you are
completely comfortable and able to relax. The best way to allow your energy to flow is to sit with your back straight in a
chair or couch. Unfortunately, a bed might be too comfortable
and you may fall asleep, and the exercises require you to be active and alert. Have a glass of water available in your space in
case you become thirsty. Place a pad and pen next to you so
that you can write down bits of spiritual wisdom as they come
into your consciousness. Burn some incense if it helps you to
feel more relaxed. You may want to have some flowers to help
beautify your space. Make sure that your space is closed off to
outside noises as best as possible. Now is the time to turn off
phones, beepers, televisions, and anything else that might disturb your quiet time. Know that you will survive without outside stimulus. Also, make sure you are wearing loose clothing

and that the temperature in your room is neither too hot nor too cold.

OPPORTUNE TIME

In order for you to receive the maximum effect of the exercise, you must commit yourself to being an active part in the healing. Therefore, you must give yourself the opportune time to do this work. It doesn't matter what time of the day you choose—morning, afternoon, or evening. If possible, it is best to be alone, so no one can disturb you. It is imperative that there are *no* outside intrusions. Reserve adequate time to do these healing processes. You *must* commit yourself to a few minutes of uninterrupted peace in order to do the exercise properly and receive the optimum benefit.

CENTER OR CENTERING

This is a process that brings the awareness of yourself to the middle part of your forehead. You do this by shutting your eyes and slowing down your breathing. Begin by taking several slow, deep breaths. Become aware of how your breath begins to relax you. Notice that you are in control of the breath, and it is not in control of you. Become aware of the feelings in your body. Start at your head and work your way down to the neck, shoulders, and arms. Note how your chest moves in and out as the lungs expand and retract. Become aware of your stomach and pelvis area. Focus on your back and hips, and then bring your awareness down into your legs and feet. As you breathe in air, visualize or sense that every molecule of air is refreshing, relaxing, renewing, and revitalizing every part of your being. See yourself "in control" of your body and mind. Relax and just be. Bring your focus to the third eye, which is located just above the bridge of your nose. You are now centered, ready for the next step.

LET GO

You will have to release or let go of various feelings, thoughts, and beliefs while you do these exercises. When you let go, the God Force energy within does the work, and you feel free of the burdens that you have been carrying. The struggle to control everything is over. At this point you will realize that everything in life moves in its own rhythm and in its own time. With this understanding, you can relax and enjoy life.

RECHARGED

After completing an exercise, you will experience a new sense of awareness. You will have a more positive outlook on life and feel more in control of your life. You will be recharged. It is important to retain this state of consciousness throughout the day, especially during the times when you feel stressed, or when you start to fall back into a pattern of self-torment.

ACTUALIZED

This is the term I use to describe your ability to actively visualize or sense yourself living and realizing your future goals. These goals may be physical, emotional, mental, or spiritual. When you are in the "actualized" state, you are fully living in the moment of the particular meditation or visualization.

MEDITATIONS

Meditation on Healing Self

Use this guided meditation to bring a sense of well-being and balance within you. The healing works on many levels at the same time, and although you may not feel a physical change, several unseen levels are being transformed. Remember that it is not enough to think or say the words, but to feel their content as well. The process is more effective when your thoughts and feelings match. When you begin a meditation, make sure that you have set up your space and have gone through the centering process.

As you sit in the chair, close your eyes and become aware of your breath, your body, and the atmosphere surrounding you. Are you comfortable? Is your mind chattering away with extraneous thoughts? If so, just acknowledge each thought and let it be. Don't judge it. Take several deep breaths, continuing to center yourself. As you go though each part of the body, imagine it relaxing and melting into *nothingness*. After this is complete, just sit and sense the peace and quiet.

Then imagine yourself floating on top of an ocean of gently moving water. Now feel the heat of an enormous bright light touching your body. The bright golden rays of this light touch every cell of your being. Feel it. Imagine that you are rising and being pulled up into this beautiful light shining above you. You are enveloped with this wonderful spiritual light and clothed in its healing vibration and unconditional love. As it gently touches every cell of your body, it brings every part of your being into proper balance and harmony. Perhaps you need some emotional healing. Sense the light creating peace and calm within you.

Let the light now illuminate the person or the situation that needs to be healed. Begin to tune into the steps necessary for forgiveness and closure. This great light restores comfort and healing where it is desired. Now see yourself being completely absorbed into the light, feeling even more peaceful. Enjoy this feeling for the next few moments.

As you come out of the light, imagine yourself in a garden called My Inner Self. The garden is made up of a variety of flowers and trees, and each one symbolizes an aspect of who you are right now and the situation in which you find yourself at this particular moment. Observe the garden. Peruse the garden. What does it look like? This garden is like a magical mirror of your inner self. It shows you what needs to be healed. Perhaps you have observed a fruit tree without fruit. This could mean that you are not "bearing fruit" or living up to your potential. Or if you see a flower that has withered on its stem, does that tell you that you need nurturing and love in order to grow?

Do you see any weeds or vines that are taking over your garden? This could represent people, situations, and things in your life that are depleting you and choking your potential for uncovering the beauty of yourself. Perhaps some of the flowers are missing petals. Ask yourself: What part of me is not complete? How can I make myself whole?

Be observant. Is there anything missing in your garden? Do you see gaping holes, or empty spaces where nothing is growing? As you meditate, ask yourself: Which flower is missing? What does that flower represent? What steps can I take to make this garden look the best it can be? What would I change to make it more enjoyable?

What do the answers tell you about yourself and your life? What lessons do you have to learn about yourself in order to grow and shine? You don't have to ask someone else for the answers. Look within and find the answers for yourself.

Now give yourself a pat on the back. Thank yourself, for today you stand at the threshold of creating a wonderful and loving garden. Now rest in complete actualized consciousness. When ready, jot down any insights from this exercise.

Meditation on Healing a Loss

No matter the type of loss, whether it is a death, the loss of a pet, the end of a job, a divorce, etc., the following meditation is designed to give you a chance to acknowledge the loss, gain insight, and discover another part of yourself.

Begin this meditation by completely setting up your space and thoroughly centering yourself. As with the first meditation, sit in a chair and close your eyes, once more becoming aware of your breath. Let each breath become more noticeable. Relax and enjoy the sensation of having nothing to do. You can just be. When your mind wanders, let it go; don't judge or analyze the thoughts that pop up. Continue to take several deep breaths, centering yourself. As you relax each body part, imagine it melting into *nothingness*. Allow a sense of peaceful quietness to permeate your whole being.

Now you are ready to visualize. See yourself sitting at the bank of a very tranquil lake. Imagine this lake and its surroundings with as many details as you choose. Maybe the water is a beautiful emerald green or a dark sapphire blue, and when you touch it, it is as warm as a bath. Tall pine trees create a beautiful frame around the lake. Perhaps you spot several majestic swans floating by. Make this setting appeal to you in whatever way you can.

When you are ready, pick out a spot on the surface of the lake. Stay focused on that spot as you envision the loss that has recently occurred in your life. If it is a person or a pet, see the image appear on the water. If it is a loss of a different kind, see the situation being lived out on the surface of the lake. Take some time to see it clearly. Feel it. Take it all in. Now, as you focus your eyes upon the lake, ask yourself: What has this loss taught me? How has it changed my life? Take a few minutes to reflect. You may want to write down what comes to mind. Ask yourself: What opportunities has this loss presented or will present to me? Give yourself time to let each opportunity come to mind. How does each opportunity make you feel? How will it change your life? Will you give yourself the patience to realize that you, and only you, can make that choice? Remember, this is your journey through life. All you need is the awareness that loss presents opportunities as stepping-stones for growth and enlightenment. Thank your loved one, or the situation, for giving you this opportunity. Thank yourself for opening your mind and heart to this information. Let go and feel recharged.

EXERCISES

Charting

This is a wonderful way to measure your progress along the road to self-empowerment and healing. You may want to purchase a binder or create your own. On a piece of paper write the date, time, and name of the exercise. Chart your feelings and reactions before you start the particular exercise. "Feeling strange" about doing a certain exercise is very common. Remember, this is new territory for most of us. Just be aware that you are beginning to take the steps necessary to heal yourself. After completing the exercise, chart the feelings that you have experienced during the exercise. Note what you would like to accomplish with the exercise in the future. It is important that you keep a progressive chart so you can track your growth.

Getting Back to You

This exercise is designed to remember a part of yourself that has been forgotten, overlooked, or unrealized. We live so much in a day-to-day survival mode that we infrequently, if ever, take the time to have a relationship with ourselves. Instead of taking charge of our lives and creating what we want, we become a pawn in life, reacting to experiences. This exercise is a necessary step to getting back to your soul's awareness.

Give yourself a certain amount of time to go through this exercise. Do not feel rushed; just enjoy the experience. You may do the exercise once and add to it, or you may do it several times. Decide what is right for your own advancement and healing. Also, do not judge or analyze the information that comes out of the exercise.

After you have established your opportune time, begin to create your space. Design it as you would a room. When you are comfortable, move to the centering process. Keep your eyes closed during the exercise, opening them only when you need to make notes.

In your mind's eye, go back to age seven or thereabouts, and try to recall a childhood memory that made you happy. Now, begin to record in your mind, or write down, the traits or characteristics that you liked most about yourself at this age. Perhaps it was your sense of humor, or your sense of adventure. Maybe there were certain people in your life who made you happy. Maybe you enjoyed a sport or hobby. Record as many positive traits as possible. Continue to move up in age and observe new revelations about yourself. What positive, fun traits pop into your mind? What do you love about yourself at these ages? What do you love doing in your free time? Who do you love being with? What is special about you? What part of life do you enjoy the most? What part of life do you want to discover when you get older?

Advance to your present age. Slowly bring yourself back to the awareness of your space. When ready, open your eyes and review your list of qualities. How many of these traits are still positive forces in your life? Are you still the same person, or have you changed? What has changed about you?

Using this list of positive traits as a guideline, redefine your priorities. Decide what you want to add to your present life and what you want to eliminate. What do you need to do to make yourself laugh and be happy? Write it down and learn from it. Last, draw a line next to the positive trait or situation you want in your life, and fill that line with two ways of accomplishing it. Recharge yourself. You are in the process of opening a treasure chest of knowledge. A new and revised self is coming alive.

Remembering Where You Came From

It is important to realize that when you suffer a major loss or transition in life, you may bring up any and *all* past losses that you never dealt with. In the process of seeing yourself as an empowered individual, in charge of your own life and destiny, you must go back and pick up where you left things hanging and not completed. When we don't have proper closure with our past, there will be lingering feelings that have an effect on our present and future life. Here is an analogy of what I mean. From time to time you have company over to your house. One of your first priorities is to get to work and put the house back in order. You walk from room to room picking up clothes, magazines, and toys, and returning them to their rightful place. You throw out the garbage and clear the sink of dirty dishes. You tidy up so your home will look presentable. Our inner house needs to be tidied up, too. When you pick up the fragments of hurt, anger, guilt, pain, etc., from the past and get rid of them, you clear the space for something new to enter. This exercise will help you to let go so you can move forward in life, feeling able to accomplish your goals.

Give yourself opportune time. Make sure to have a pad and pen by your side to write down any revelations that you discover during the exercise. Center yourself. Go back once again in age to the first time you remember a loss. This could be as minor as someone taking a toy away. Experience the feelings you had when the toy was taken from you. Are you angry? Are you frightened? Are you confused? Let your feelings rise to the surface and acknowledge them. What did the experience teach you? Did you throw a temper tantrum? Did you get quiet and withdrawn? Did you cry? Did you run and hide? Did you whine? Is this behavior familiar to you in the present? Write about your feelings or actually verbalize them. If you are angry at someone, such as your parent, tell him now, at this moment, how you feel. Let your feelings out. Don't judge your feelings, just let them be.

Now progress in age. As you do, you may notice that the losses becoming more complex. They could include your parents' divorce or changing schools. Whatever you experience, feel it, express it, and let go. Bring yourself to the present time. What loss are you dealing with now? Are you reacting as you did as a child or teen? Perhaps there are several losses you are experiencing at once. Write them down and express how you feel about them.

You may have to do this exercise several times to fully experience all the feelings that were never expressed. Never sell yourself short. Your feelings are valid and important. Let go and recharge.

Letter Writing

Prepare your space. Have a pad, pen, and envelope available. Center yourself and be prepared to work. When you are ready, start writing a letter to the person who has passed, or to the situation that is your loss. Describe exactly how you are feeling and what you want the deceased person to know. Write how this loss has changed your life. Express everything, including any anger or blame you might have repressed.

After you have completed the letter, review it to make sure that everything is covered. Now place it in an envelope, seal it, and write the name or the situation on it. Place the envelope in a safe place. In a couple of days, repeat the exercise, but instead of writing to someone, or about something, write a letter in response to your original. When you are thoroughly finished with the response, seal it in another envelope and place it with the first letter. Two days later, take out both letters and open them up in the order in which they were written. Notice the difference in your present feelings about the loss. Begin to evaluate your changes. Let go and recharge.

Create Your Future Now

Once again prepare your space and center yourself. You are about to create a game plan for a new life and new routines. Make a list in your binder of where you would like to see yourself in the next five years. What changes would you like to make? What relationships would you like to have? How would things be different? Actualize. On a new sheet of paper, create another list of things that you would want to accomplish or do if you learned that you had a terminal illness and a limited amount of time on this earth. In other words, live tomorrow as though it were your last day. How would you change? What would you accomplish? How would your life be different? Compare both lists. Notice the similarities and differences. This will give you a clearer definition of what you want and what you need. Let go and recharge.

 ## SIMPLE EXERCISES TO HELP YOU HEAL

- Set up a shrine for a loved one that has passed over. Place pictures, poems, and the person's favorite mementos.
- Begin new activities. Challenge yourself with doing things that you have always wanted to do. Perhaps it is a cooking or gardening class. Begin to fill your time with things that you love to do.
- Make a list of ten things you do that make life harder for yourself. Make some sort of an effort to slowly take those items off the list. Take your time. You don't have to do everything in a day. Replace the eliminated items with things that make life easier for you.
- Plant a tree, garden, or flower bed for the one you love.
- Carry on your loved one's memory by finishing an activity that he or she started but wasn't able to complete.
- Put yourself on a "health routine" and give your body goals to achieve. Join a gym or start a yoga class.
- Make a list of things that make you laugh. Know that the person who passed would want you to be happy.
- Write down your feelings each day in a journal or diary.
- Don't judge yourself for one whole day, and notice how you feel.

- Say something nice to a stranger today.
- Get active once again. Join a group or volunteer.
- Give someone a hug today.
- Smile at as many people as you can today.
- Reorganize the house. Throw out the old to make a place for the new.
- Express your creativity. Redesign a room in your house, or write a book.
- Understand that grief is awesome and a bigger power than you. You will cry and be depressed when you least suspect it. It is okay.
- Remember that everyone grieves differently, and some not at all. Each of us is a unique, individualistic creature of God.
- Forgive yourself for being upset or angry. The most important thing is to feel. It is okay if someone else doesn't understand your hurt.
- You are not alone. Surround yourself with others who have gone through the process of grief.
- Make a list of the opportunities this loss has provided you. How have you changed others' lives?
- Acknowledge your connection with deceased loved ones by celebrating their birthdays and the anniversaries of their deaths in whatever way you choose.
- Light a candle for the one you love. Light one for yourself.
- Accept responsibility for your life.
- Get a little more sleep and look forward to your dreams.
- Get a massage.
- Enjoy a glass of expensive wine.
- Read those books you have been putting off.
- Rent several movies, pop some popcorn, and have a good time with your own company.

SPIRIT
ENLIGHTENMENT

*O*ver the years I have received thousands of letters from people around the
world. People usually want to know how
they can communicate with their loved ones
in spirit, how to get through the grieving,
and if they will ever heal. In this chapter I will
answer some of the more frequently asked
questions. You may find that a similar situation pertains to your life. In sharing the wisdom from my guides and those on the other
side in heaven, my desire is that you can get
back to living your life with an added awareness of loss and grieving.

Q: Who greets us when we leave our bodies and go to the spirit world?

A: It is different for each soul, but most commonly your parents, grandparents, children, other family members, and friends meet you. Any person who has shared an affinity or love bond with you during your recent earth life will greet you. Spirit guides will also meet you and gently assist you with the transition. There may also be other spirits whom you may recognize from prior lifetimes and experiences on earth.

Q: Why do people who are dead appear in our dreams? Is it really them or a figment of our imagination?

A: Dreaming of departed loved ones is the most common way spirits communicate with those on earth. When we are in a state of sleep, our rational mind-sets are no longer in control, and cannot make judgments or criticisms as they do when we are awake. Instead they are bypassed, and the door is open to other levels of consciousness. During the sleep period your spirit body travels in the astral levels and is able to contact and communicate with your spirit family. Our brain interprets these perceptions as dreams.

Q: What other ways do spirits try to communicate?

A: It is quite common for spirits to manipulate electricity in various ways. For instance, they are able to cause lightbulbs to flicker, telephones to ring, radios and televisions to turn on and off. Many times the deceased's perfume or aftershave lotion fills the air. This usually means that your loved one's spirit is around you.

Q: *How long does it take a spirit to fully realize that it is dead?*

A: There are many factors involved here. First, it depends on how a person passed. Prolonged illness, which depletes the body's energy, is a factor. Such a spirit will take a little longer to recharge with life-force energy when it passes. If someone dies suddenly, with no lingering illness, his or her restorative time is more instantaneous. Second, a person with a belief system that embraces life after death adapts more easily to the spirit dimensions. A person who doesn't believe in eternal life will have a more difficult time adjusting to his or her new life. However, after a while a spirit will begin to recognize its home once again and understand what has occurred. There is no such thing as time in the spiritual dimensions, so what is considered a day here may be a minute there.

Q: *Do deceased spirits miss us like we miss them?*

A: Of course they do. Love bonds never die. Unlike us, however, spirits are back home in heaven, looking at earth life from a different dimension. Since they no longer have to fear death, their awareness is changed. Often our loved ones painfully attempt to communicate with us not to grieve for them anymore. They want us to know that they are still fully alive.

Q: *Is it possible to speak to a child who is stillborn?*

A: That depends. If a spirit has already found another vehicle in which to reincarnate, it may not be able to communicate. However, I have brought through many spirits who were aborted and stillborn. They usually come through with the assistance of a relative or a child caretaker.

Q: *Since my wife died, I can't concentrate on anything. Will this change?*

A: Yes. You are still in shock, and this stage of grief can last for some time. Do not attempt to do too much at this time; just take it easy and feel your loss. Your feelings are a testament to the love that you both shared with each other. In time you will begin to get used to a new regimen in your life, and you will go on. But it does make life easier when you realize that your wife is with you and watching over you, although in a different form.

Q: *Why would our son be taken away at such a young age?*

A: First of all, the soul is ageless. You have to realize that this earth is our schoolroom, affording us incredible opportunities for spiritual growth and learning. Sometimes a soul leaves "early," in "tragic" or "untimely" circumstances. This is how it appears to us in our limited physical understanding. But in such a situation, a soul, or the family, had to learn something from the experience. What has his death taught you? Of what opportunities has it availed you? The soul may also be working out past-life karma. This means it had to balance actions from a previous existence. Everything on earth is played out or experienced solely for our soul's growth.

Q: *If our loved ones have passed on and have chosen to reincarnate, how is it possible to contact them in spirit?*

A: As spirits, we are not limited to a physical body and a physical time frame. The physical body is one of many bodies that you possess. A soul exists on many different levels all at once because it has multidimensional awareness. Therefore, a larger part of you exists in another dimension. That said, I have found that a "part" of the earthly personality remains intact to a degree in spirit. This makes it possible to contact your loved ones who passed. As part of a "soul group," you are able to connect with this part of spirit.

Q: *When does a soul choose to reincarnate again?*

A: A soul chooses a moment in time that is best suited for its spiritual growth. In other words, it chooses situations in a coming earthly life that will afford it the best opportunities for much needed learning. The decision to return to earth is completely left up to a soul's free will.

Q: *Is there evil? What happens to evil people who pass over, like Hitler, for instance?*

A: We are all a part of the God consciousness. Therefore, we have free will to use it in whatever way we choose. Good and evil are what we make of our choices. Light and dark can be used to describe our consciousness. Many times, as a soul goes through its evolution, it must tap into many aspects of its human nature in order to understand all possibilities. Therefore, a soul will try all different situations in which to learn and grow. In the spiritual dimensions there seems to be no judgment, only an awareness, of these situations. In the end, every thought, word, and deed will be accounted for by that soul. However, many souls are stuck in a lower vibration of consciousness that manifests in depravity and baseness. When a soul creates mass destruction and horror, like Hitler, and leaves the physical realm, it will gravitate to an existence that is shared by others who have a similar "dark" consciousness.

Q: *When spirits come through, why can't they tell us more interesting things instead of mentioning items that seem trivial?*

A: First of all, spirits communicate messages that you are able to understand. If they were to discuss spiritual life as they know it, you would have no reference point from which to relate. It would be as if they were speaking a foreign language. Second, spirits go back to "yesterday's memory," and they attempt to bring through thoughts about things that you both understand. Remember, spirits are outside of our linear time-frame. Because they live in a world of thought, everything is speeded up and is instantaneous. They must send simple thoughts and "feelings" for us to understand. To some the information may seem trivial, but to the person receiving the message, it is the proof he or she needs to know that a loved one still exists.

Q: Can a medium contact anyone whom the sitter desires?

A: No. Any medium who says she or he can is incorrect. Like humans, there are many spirits that are not very good at communicating. While others are not able to manifest their ideas through the corresponding vibration. There are still others who may not want to respond to this heavy, earthly condition because it reminds them of their death, and they don't want to "relive" that memory, especially if the death was very traumatic or draining. Think of how you would react. Would you want to experience something unpleasant over and over again?

Q: Are all suicides condemned to hell?

A: No. There is so such thing as "hell" as a place of fire and damnation from which we can never depart. The spirit dimensions are not places but states of consciousness. When a soul cannot learn its lessons and leaves through suicide, it returns home. It may stay in a "reflective" state for a period of adjustment. A soul who commits suicide is never harmed or condemned to "hell."

Q: *Is it possible to contact my loved one who passed over without the use of a medium?*

A: Yes. You can begin to sit in daily meditation and learn to become more sensitive to the spiritual world. You will need a lot of patience to learn to "listen" to the subtle feelings and thoughts of spirit. You may also work and communicate with spirits in your dreams. However, not everyone possesses the degree of sensitivity and clarity necessary to communicate or "hear" the higher frequencies to which a medium is accustomed.

Q: *Can anybody be a medium?*

A: No. Every person possesses a certain level of psychic or intuitive ability that can be developed and utilized. There are degrees of sensitivity and ability, and I believe that a medium is a bit more sensitive than most. I like to compare it to playing the piano. Everyone can learn to play, but not everyone is a concert pianist.

Q: *What effect does a skeptical mind have on a reading?*

A: Thought is energy. Energy is real and creates degrees of atomic movement. Doubt is negative energy that tears down rather than builds up. Skeptical or negative thoughts create conditions that are almost impossible for the spirit forces to puncture. No matter how strong a medium may be, the thoughts of a skeptical sitter create a very dense atmosphere of energy. It is much easier for a spirit to come through a vibration of a higher mind-set, such as love, which strengthens the atmospheric conditions rather than depletes them.

Q: *My mother didn't speak English when she was alive. Can a medium still get a message from her?*

A: Yes. Communication from spirits is not limited to language but thoughts, and thoughts are universal in language.

Q: *Does my dead mother know what I am thinking?*

A: Yes. Spirits are more akin to mental thoughts, since they reside in a mental world. Therefore, spirits can understand all your thoughts and feel all your prayers.

Q: *Where is heaven or the spirit world located?*

A: You must realize that your body, and the so-called physical world, is not as solid as your five senses would have you believe. Because the energy vibration of the physical world is so slow, the energy appears to be solid. However, we are constantly bombarded by radio and television waves that pass through solid matter. This energy vibrates at a different frequency, which appears to be invisible. So while our bodies move through a solid, physical world of time and space, our minds and souls actually vibrate in another invisible dimension, which interpenetrate our bodies. Therefore, your mind and soul are living in a spirit world and will always live there. When we die, we begin to become aware of this new dimension of existence, or "spirit world." When we say that heaven is already within us, it means the spirit world exists in and through you already. It is not a "place" to which we must go.

Q: *What do I tell my child about death?*

A: In many ways, children can adapt more easily to death than adults, and understand a lot more than we give them credit for. First of all, let them know that it is okay to cry and miss the person they loved. Second, guide them through the grief stages, and let them know what they might expect. Don't lie to them or give them false hope. Third, children respond better to love and encouragement. Help them to realize that life on earth is a lot like school, and that we have to learn some lessons that may be more difficult than others, such as the loss of someone they love. Last, assure them that in time they will feel better, and that their loved one is with them in a different way.

Q: *I have lost my husband and my will to live. What can I do?*

A: First, understand that you are going through a grief process, and you will feel devastated at times. Second, find someone to talk to so that you can express your feelings. Third of all, when you are calm, reevaluate your situation. Begin to ask yourself what your husband would have wanted you to do. Would he want you to give up on life, or take hold of it and create a happier situation? Realize that this is a major change in your life. You will never forget it, nor will it last forever. You will go on and experience more of life. Give yourself time to get to know yourself once again. What you find may change the way you feel.

Q: *My son died in a plane crash. Was it painful? How do I know he is okay?*

A: I have worked with many people whose loved ones have died in tragic circumstances such as this one. On each of these occasions a spirit has come through and relayed the fact that it lost consciousness before the impact and cannot remember the actual moment of the crash. I believe that it is God's way of protecting us. A part of our consciousness shuts off or "freezes" when these types of deaths occur, and a person feels no pain.

Q: *I've been having a difficult time with my teenage boy since his father died. He doesn't want to talk about it. What can I do?*

A: Encourage him to talk to his friends. Reassure him that you are not going anywhere. Let him know that you are available to talk whenever he chooses. Just knowing that you are there helps him to feel less isolated and afraid. You can also ask him if he would like to speak to someone outside the family, such as a therapist. If he cannot express himself verbally, perhaps he can show his feelings in other ways, through music or painting, or some sports activity or hobby. Give him the time he needs to grieve, and remember that everyone goes through loss and grief in his own way.

Q: *I didn't have time to tell my father I loved him before he died, and now I feel guilty. How can I let him know how I feel?*

A: You can speak to him out loud or in your thoughts. Spirit is very connected to our mental thoughts and hears them all the time. You may also want to write him a letter and express your feelings to him in this way. Most important, stop beating up on yourself. You need to be respectful and loving to yourself during this difficult time.

Q: *How long do people usually grieve?*

A: Each person grieves differently depending upon emotional makeup and his or her relationship with the loss. A person who loses a husband may have a different type of grief than someone who loses a house. Never expect that you will get over it overnight. That is highly unlikely. Grieving is a process. Acknowledge it, and learn from it.

Q: *Are there different heavens for different religions?*

A: Heaven is composed of many levels. The level into which we enter right after we die is very much like our earthly existence. We still use our human religious beliefs to guide and nourish us. People of like minds gravitate together and share an affinity in these spirit dimensions. Eventually all souls evolve from these earth-like levels. They become aware that religion is a human tool, and it is not needed in the higher planes, where the only "religion" is love.

Q: *Is it easier to contact spirits who have recently departed?*

A: Generally, yes. However, there is an acclimatization period that spirits must first go through, and very recently departed ones are too involved with "settling in" to communicate with loved ones on earth. Conversely, the longer a loved one is in the spirit world, the less it identifies with its last incarnation. Therefore, it becomes more difficult to communicate with such a spirit.

Q: *How is religion beneficial?*

A: Paths of Light, or religions, can assist people to open their heart centers and their connection to the higher consciousness or "God consciousness." Most religions emanate from good intentions. However, when religions become polluted by man's ego, desire for power, control over others, and material wealth, they become imbued with fear, and use fear to attract a flock. Like the fallen angels, religions that operate from this level descend to the lowest part of consciousness.

Q: *Do you use the Bible when you help others?*

A: I believe the Bible is a great tool. The difficulty in using the Bible is to comprehend its true meaning without inflicting man's erroneous interpretations upon it. Simple truths are the key to spirituality. The Golden Rule of "Do unto others as you would have them do unto you" is from the Bible, and I use this teaching all the time in my work with people.

Q: Is the Ouija board bad to use?

A: When used properly, and under the right conditions, the Ouija board is a wonderful tool to become aware of your spiritual self. When used as a game, and with the wrong intentions, it can be misguiding and even dangerous. Remember that you are opening yourself to levels of consciousness of which you are unaware. One must be properly familiar with what he or she does before getting involved in any form of psychic phenomenon.

Q: How does one get rid of bad karma?

A: By beginning to live your life with a "conscious awareness." You must be completely responsible for your thoughts and actions in everyday life. By living this way, you become in charge of your life instead of reacting to situations and circumstances. Thus you begin to do the right thing in all your affairs. This is the only way to begin to balance out the "bad" karma. Remember that karma is a reaction to actions, and what you put out, you get back in some way or other. The choice is ours to make, and it can either be "good" or "bad."

Q: My son was mentally ill on earth. Will he carry that over when he passes into spirit?

A: The spirit body is perfect. The condition of mental illness is an aspect of the physical world. A soul will usually choose this circumstance to develop itself or to teach others about love.

Q: My daughter died from an overdose of drugs. I feel so guilty and keep on thinking I could have prevented it. I blame myself for her death. How can I get through this?

A: Stop playing God. You probably did the best you could in the circumstances in which you found yourself. Your daughter must be responsible for her actions. As parents we can encourage our children to keep out of danger, but it is up to them to make their own decisions. It's understandable that you wonder what you could have done to prevent such a tragedy, but you have to learn to think differently. Think instead of all the good things that you did for your daughter, and how important you were to her life. Realize how fortunate you both were to share in each other's lives. She will continue to grow in spirit. You must finish your work here on earth, and when it is your time, you will join her in heaven.

Q: *Do people who are addicted to drugs, alcohol, or tobacco lose this addiction when they pass into spirit?*

A: Not right away. A spirit arrives with the exact same mind-set that it had on earth. In time, however, a spirit will realize that it no longer needs to have these things in order to feel happy or satisfied. A spirit will arrive at this new awareness in its own time.

Q: *My wife and I lost our home in a fire, and we are very angry. What can I do to help us both get over this loss?*

A: Realize that you will move through it. Attempt to use your anger in positive ways. There are many people who have turned a tragedy like yours into something beneficial for many people, like the mothers who started MADD. Give yourself enough time to adjust to your new situation. Nothing changes overnight. Realize that your memories will always be a part of you. Look forward to the day when you can create a new home and can begin new memories and experiences in it.

Q: *If you don't believe in life after death, what happens to you when you die?*

A: A spirit guide meets these unaware spirits and assists them to understand their new expression of life. Many times they have to be shown proof that they died, and will often visit their own funerals. Sometimes these pour souls frantically attempt to contact their living relatives. When they realize that no one can hear or see them, they begin to resign themselves to the fact that they have survived death. Slowly they become aware that they are still alive in another form. They begin to feel regret for their close-minded beliefs while on earth. They recognize many missed opportunities because of their limited thinking. There are many spirits that will help to give these tortured souls love and guidance.

Q: *How would you describe God?*
A: God is a term for pure and unconditional Love. It is the Universal force, the All, and the everything. The Life of God is manifest in every single atom. This force is the supreme expression of life itself. Each one of us is a spark of this God Force energy. It is really impossible to fully comprehend God in our limited and dense physical vibration. Love is the closest description I can give.

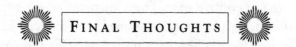

FINAL THOUGHTS

I have written this book to comfort and assist you in resolving various questions or circumstances of your daily life. It is not meant to be a quick fix for your heartache, but to bring you some clarity in the way you think about a situation. Life is a journey made up of many twists and turns. How we react to a particular situation will either assist or hinder us. Each of us comes to this planet with the intent to learn about ourselves through interacting with others. Many times we place ourselves in difficult and unbearable situations, but these are the ones that help us to grow the most. Your losses are your experiences of life. Realize that these losses give you a new understanding and awareness of yourself. Use this awareness to serve others, for that is the soul's nature. Look at these difficult circumstances as stepping-stones and create something positive from them. Have courage to start anew, and to love as much as you can. Now is the time to make the most of the rest of the moments of your life.

HEALING RESOURCES

GROUPS AND ASSOCIATIONS

The Samaritans
A service offering confidential support through emotional crisis (24 hours per day).
Tel: 0345 90 90 90

Foundation for the Study of Infant Deaths
Foundation for the Study of Infant Deaths (FSID) is the UK's leading cot death charity. Phone the 24 hour helpline for advice and information.
Head Office: Artillery House, 11–19 Artillery Row,
London, SW1P 1RT,
United Kingdom
24 hour helpline: 020 7233 2090
General enquiries: 020 7222 8001
Fax: 020 7222 8002
Email: *fsid@sids.org.uk*
Website: http://www.sids.org.uk/fsid/

Cruse Bereavement Care
A counselling service to help individuals and families through the emotions and practical problems of bereavement.
126 Sheen Road, Richmond, TW9 1UR,
United Kingdom
Tel: 020 8940 4818

Road Peace

Provides practical and emotional help to those newly bereaved
and injured as a result of a road crash.

PO Box 2579, London, NW10 3PW,
United Kingdom
Tel: 020 8838 5102
Support line: 020 8964 1021
Fax: 020 8838 5103
Email: *info@roadpeace.org.uk*

Natural Death Centre

The Natural Death Centre is a non-profit charitable project
launched in Britain in 1991. It aims to support those dying at
home and their carers and to help them arrange funerals. Its more
general aim is to help improve 'the quality of dying'.

20 Heber Road, London, NW2 6AA,
United Kingdom
Tel: 020 8208 2853
Fax: 020 8452 6434
Email: *rhino@dial.pipex.com*
Website: www.naturaldeath.org.uk

Support after Murder and Manslaughter

SAMM offers understanding and support to families and friends
who have been bereaved as a result of murder and manslaughter
through mutual support of others who have suffered a similar
tragedy.

National Office: Cranmer House, 39 Brixton Road,
London, SW9 6DZ,
United Kingdom
Tel: 020 7735 3838
Fax: 020 7735 3900
Email: *samm@ukpeople.net*

Terence Higgins Trust

Organisation offering counselling for those affected by HIV and
AIDS.

52 Greys Inn Road, London, WC1X 8JU,
United Kingdom
Tel: 020 7831 0330

The Compassionate Friends

A nation wide self help group of parents whose child of any age, has died from any cause.

53 North Street, Bristol, BS3 1EN,
United Kingdom
Tel: 0117 953 9639

National Association of Widows

Offers advice and support for widows, holding group meetings on a national level.

54 Allison Street, Digbeth, Birmingham, B5 5TH,
United Kingdom
Tel: 01334 655903

Internet Healing Resources

Http://www.griefnet.co.uk
Http://www.webhealing.com
Http://www.petloss.com
Http://www.bereavement.org.uk
Http://www.sids.org.uk

BIBLIOGRAPHY

General

Crenshaw, David A. *Bereavement: Counseling the Grieving Through the Life Cycle*. New York: Crossroad, 1990.

Katafiasz, Karen. *Grief Therapy*. Saint Meinrad, IN: Abbey Press, 1993.

Markham, Ursula. *Element Guide to Bereavement: Your Questions Answered*. Boston: Element Books, 1996.

O'Connor, Nancy. *Letting Go with Love: The Grieving Process*. Tucson, AZ: La Mariposa Press, 1985.

Ray, Veronica. *Choosing Happiness: The Art of Living Unconditionally*. Center City, MN: Hazelden Information and Educational Services, 1990.

Shaw, Eva. *What to Do When a Loved One Dies*. Irvine, CA: Dickens Press, 1994.

Tatelbaum, Judy. *The Courage to Grieve*. New York: Harper-Collins, 1984.

White Eagle. *Beautiful Road Home: Living in the Knowledge That You Are in Spirit*. White Eagle Publishing Trust, P.O. Box 550, Marina del Rey, CA 90294-0550.

White Eagle. *Sunrise: A Book of Knowledge and Comfort for the Bereaved*. White Eagle Publishing Trust, P.O. Box 550, Marina del Rey, CA 90294-0550.

Children/Teenagers

Fitzgerald, Helen. *The Grieving Child: A Parent's Guide*. New York: Simon & Schuster, 1992.

Sanders, Catherine M. *How to Survive the Loss of a Child: Filling the Emptiness and Rebuilding Your Life*. Rocklin, CA: Prima Publishing, 1992.

Schuurman, Donna L. *Helping Children Cope with Death*. Dougy Center, P.O. Box 86852, Portland, OR 97286.

Trozzi, Maria, and Kathy Massimini. *Talking with Children about Loss*. New York: Berkley, 1999.

Divorce

Everett, Craig, and Sandra V. Everett. *Healthy Divorce*. San Francisco: Jossey-Bass, 1998.

McWade, Micki. *Getting Up, Getting Over, Getting On: A Twelve-Step Guide to Divorce Recovery*. Beverly Hills, CA: Champion Press, 1999.

Webb, Dwight. *Divorce and Separation Recovery: Ten Stages of Grieving Relationship, Loss, and Finding Yourself*. Portsmouth, NH: Peter E. Randall, 1996.

Pets

Hanna, Jack. *Jack Hanna's Ultimate Guide to Pets*. New York: Berkley, 1998.

Sife, Wallace. *The Loss of a Pet*. New York: Howell Books, 1998.

Also by James Van Praagh

Talking to Heaven: A medium's message of life after death

Part spiritual memoir and part instructional guide, *Talking to Heaven* offers a powerful and inspirational message about the world beyond. James Van Praagh shows us a means of dealing with sorrow and loss in a positive way. He shows how you can contact the spirit world on your own, recognise your spirit guides and become aware of the 'spirit signs' that loved ones are sending you here on earth. Filled with hope and enlightenment about our spiritual future, it is a book that will change the way you look at death – and life.

Reaching to Heaven: A Spiritual Journey through Life and Death

Reaching to Heaven is an enriching and uplifting guide to becoming a true spiritual being. James Van Praagh takes you on an inspirational journey that will allow you to understand what happens at death, what the spirit world is like, how a soul chooses to be reborn, and how the actual process of reincarnation works. *Reaching to Heaven* includes moving stories of after-death communication and simple exercises and meditations that will help us to rediscover our true spiritual nature and achieve self-awareness, self-worth and self-love.